Family Support

# Family Support

## Prevention, Early Intervention and Early Help

Nick Frost, Shaheen Abbott and
Tracey Race

polity

First published in 2015 by Polity Press

Polity Press
65 Bridge Street
Cambridge CB2 1UR, UK

Polity Press
350 Main Street
Malden, MA 02148, USA

ISBN-13: 978-0-7456-7259-5
ISBN-13: 978-0-7456-7260-1(pb)

A catalogue record for this book is available from the British Library.

Library of Congress Cataloging-in-Publication Data

Frost, Nick, 1953–
    Family support : prevention, early intervention and early help / Nick Frost, Shaheen Abbott, Tracey Race.
        pages cm
    Includes bibliographical references and index.
    ISBN 978-0-7456-7259-5 (hardback : alk. paper) -- ISBN 978-0-7456-7260-1 (pbk. : alk. paper) 1. Family services. 2. Family social work. 3. Families. I. Abbott, Shaheen. II. Race, Tracey. III. Title.
    HV697.F76 2015
    362.82'53--dc23
                            2015004490

Typeset in 9.5 on 12 pt Utopia by
Servis Filmsetting Ltd, Stockport, Cheshire
Printed and bound in the UK by CPI Group (UK) Ltd, Croydon, CR0 4YY

For further information on Polity, visit our website:
politybooks.com

# Contents

# Acknowledgements

*NF*: Thanks to Andy Lloyd, Fiona Abram, Hannah Burgess, Sue Elmer and Richard Skues for help with various aspects of this book. Thanks to Dawn for all your support.

*SA*: Thank you to my copiously patient husband, Bryn. Thank you to the families, to those who work with them and continue to believe in fighting for them. Thank you to my team in Leeds, who demonstrate this daily, with unrelenting strength and respect.

*TR*: Appreciation for the support of my family and also to the social work team at Leeds Beckett University.

# Introduction

The idea of 'prevention' has been an essential element of child welfare practice since its Victorian origins (Stedman Jones 1976): what has changed over the years has been the way the aim of 'preventing' the emergence of social and family problems has been conceptualized in policy and then put into practice. These changes are reflected in family support 'projects' aimed at preventing family breakdown and related social problems; such projects include the Victorian National Society for the Prevention of Cruelty to Children (NSPCC), the post-Second World War Family Service Units, the New Labour Sure Start initiative and the contemporary 'Troubled Families' programme. Such initiatives reflect changing ideologies about, and approaches to, family support. These ideologies are also reflected in shifting terminology – from 'prevention' through to contemporary debates about 'family support, 'early intervention' and 'early help'. These important conceptual issues will be discussed and dissected in the opening chapters of this book and will inform the rest of our policy and practice analysis.

Surprisingly little has been written about 'family support', especially in the form of texts suitable for students and/or books which focus on how to actually plan, organize and deliver family support. One aim of this book is to address this gap by producing a readable, accessible and practical text aimed at outlining and explaining current theory, policy, research and practice relating to 'family support'. We aim to make a contribution to the rehabilitation of 'family support' as a concept and as a practice: we want to argue strongly in favour of the crucial role of family support which in recent years has been displaced by the predominant safeguarding and child protection agenda (see Featherstone, White and Morris 2014).

This book is made up of chapters which can be read independently, but which as a whole are intended to provide a comprehensive overview of family support theory, policy, practice and research. One aim of the book is to help future and current child welfare professionals extend their use of theory and research to inform their practice within a changing and complex multi-agency context.

The book is designed for all those professionals involved in child welfare and safeguarding education and training at undergraduate and postgraduate levels, as well as at more experienced practitioners progressing towards post-qualifying awards or those in practice who want to inform their family support practice. In recent years, there has been a growth in degree-level programmes with titles such as Child and Family Studies, or indeed Family Support Studies, for which this may be a core book. We also hope that the book will be of interest to academics, researchers and policy makers alike.

Whilst this book is part of a series aimed primarily at social workers we contend that family support is essentially multi-disciplinary or indeed trans-disciplinary. Social workers do have a key role: we hope they can apply some of the approaches discussed here in all their work, including safeguarding and looked-after children work (Frost and Parton 2009). The role of family support has however been displaced from social work to a myriad of other settings and professions and para-professionals, so we hope the book is of interest, for example, to youth workers, play workers, community health staff, children centre staff and many others.

The book stresses the existence of a continuum in relation to family support practice – from universal family support through to the targeted safeguarding of vulnerable children and young people. This continuum reflects that, while all families require some sort of support in raising their children, some identified families will be recognized as families with 'children in need' or as 'troubled families', while a smaller number will receive family support as part of a child protection plan. The book draws on restorative practices – those that are high on support but are also authoritative in providing clear limits and boundaries (see http://www.irrp.edu/).

The eight features of family support outlined below have underpinned our analysis in this book.

1.  Family support offers inclusive and engaging practices based on the idea of offering support to families and children who feel they require it. Family support is therefore strongly suggestive of partnership, engagement and consent.
2.  Such support can be offered early in the life of the child or early in the emergence of the identified challenge facing the family. It is important that family support services can be relevant to all children and young people, and not only to younger children.
3.  Family support is a proactive process which engages with the parent(s) and/or young person in a process of change. Implicit in the term 'family support' is the suggestion of bringing about change within the family network.
4.  Family support attempts to prevent the emergence, or worsening, of family challenges.
5.  Family support is necessarily based in a theory of change. Any family support intervention should aim to result in some desirable change, and it draws on a belief that change is achievable.
6.  Family support draws on a diverse 'tool kit' of skills and approaches. It attempts to develop and encourage local, informal support networks.
7.  Family support aims to generate wider social change and benefits. Such results may lead to a saving in public expenditure, a decrease

in social problems, an improvement in the quality of family life or a reduction in measurable outcomes, such as the number of children coming into care.

8.  Family support works with children and young people in partnership and encourages and develops their resilience.

These eight principles will inform core arguments and practice suggestions made throughout this book.

We strongly support the deployment of the term 'family support'. Writing in 2006, Dolan, Canavan and Pinkerton argued that: 'Family support has become a major strategic orientation in services for children and families. It now occupies a significant place within the array of care and welfare interventions' (2006: 11). At the time of writing this book (2015), we are concerned that this 'strategic orientation' is becoming lost as we are concerned about the predominant use of the terms 'early help', and in particular 'early intervention', as they tend to:

*   devalue the 'support' element of family support;
*   draw on a restrictive model of research that suggests that all interventions can be measured;
*   promote early intervention which is particularly authoritarian in nature;
*   promote short-term, time-limited programmes, as opposed to ongoing responsive support;
*   emphasize 'early' years programmes as opposed to support through the whole of childhood.

The book draws on international research and other data to inform our argument: inevitably, given our geographical base, the reader may observe that much of the material is drawn from England. It is difficult to accurately reflect the variations of policy and legislation across the United Kingdom, where England, Scotland, Wales and Northern Ireland all have differing degrees of devolution (see our Resources section for guidance on this). As a result, child welfare and family support differ across the four jurisdictions: we have attempted to provide examples from all four nations. In general, however, we would argue that, once local detail is placed to one side, most of the material has implications across regional and national boundaries.

## The structure of the book

This volume is divided into three parts. In Part I, Understanding Family Support, we address three different contextual elements:

*   social history, political context and theories of 'family support';
*   the contemporary political context;
*   the challenges of researching and measuring 'family support'.

In chapter 1, the social history, context of and definitions and theories of 'family support' are explored. Family support has a long history which dates back, at least in the United Kingdom, to Victorian times. The roots of family support, for example, can be found in the early work of the National Society for the Prevention of Cruelty to Children (NSPCC). As we will discuss, the early SPCC inspectors utilized court proceedings and sometimes removed children, but their predominant approach was to reform family life (Ferguson 2004). Further historical roots are explored before we move to examine the definitions of both 'family' and 'support'. Both 'family' and 'support' are explored as contested and complex concepts, which must underpin our understanding of this area of practice. Differing theoretical approaches to 'family' are explored, presented and analysed. A technique for understanding family support will be developed, based on the primary, secondary, tertiary and quaternary framework devised in the 1970s by Hardiker et al.

Chapter 2 explores the broader context of family support work. All forms of child welfare practice have political and ideological elements, and this is certainly the case in relation to family support, which is inseparable from key political debates about welfare, the role of the state, the family and childhood. The impact of social and economic policies on families and family breakdown is explored. This leads to a discussion of contemporary debates about the utilization of 'prevention', 'family support', 'early help' and 'early intervention'. The relevance of this debate to students, researchers and policy makers is explained and analysed.

Chapter 3 explores the challenges of researching family support. Family support, it is claimed, offers particular challenges to research in terms of measuring success and outcomes. Differing approaches to research have been adopted across the globe with differing underpinning methodologies. The advantages of randomized controlled trials (RCTs) and more qualitative approaches are explored and explained. Specific research projects, demonstrating differing approaches, are presented. A detailed case study of the recent LARC studies is provided.

Having developed a historical, political and research context for family support in Part II, Delivering Family Support, we explore specific approaches to family support, including an examination of:

- community-based projects;
- home visiting;
- parenting education;
- targeted approaches;
- relationship-based practice;
- family group conferences.

We do not suggest that these approaches make up the whole of 'family support' but that these six forms of practice make essential contributions to family support as a system, which encompasses a range of approaches.

In chapter 4, we explore community-based approaches to family support. In many ways, this is the 'soul' of family support, offering grass-roots, universal and non-stigmatizing services to families in local areas. The advantages and disadvantages of such universal programmes based on community development and participation will be explored, drawing on research and practice examples. A case study of such approaches will be presented.

In chapter 5, 'home visiting' is explored, which is often a key element of family support programmes, including for example Home-Start and Perry High Scope. The nature of home visiting will be explored, including some of the extensive research carried out in this field. Some of the issues around volunteer and professional approaches to home visiting will be presented.

In chapter 6, programmes for parenting education, which stands both independently and as part of more comprehensive family support, are explored. The differing schools of parenting education will be discussed and the research findings are presented in relation to key programmes, such as Webster Stratton and Triple P. The debates about whether parenting education should be universal or targeted are outlined and discussed. A case study of the role of parenting education is provided and analysed.

The universal approaches explored in chapter 4 will be contrasted with more targeted approaches in chapter 7, usually at the 'secondary' or 'tertiary' level of intervention, and often aimed at combatting issues such as domestic violence and substance abuse. The complex issues around targeting and identifying potentially 'troubled' families are discussed. The authors provide and analyse a case study that illustrates the debates around 'targeted approaches'.

In chapter 8, the nature of the relationship in family support and the centrality of this to family support is explored and analysed. We argue for the importance of this approach and that it is in danger of being undermined by more programme-based initiatives. Again, a case study is presented and analysed.

In chapter 9, family group conferences (FGCs) are discussed: they form a crucial and increasingly utilized element of family support programmes. The developing research in this field will be presented. The differing findings of studies related to 'outcomes' are analysed and the reasons for inconsistent findings debated. The links of FGCs with the 'restorative practice' movement will be outlined and critically analysed. A case study of an FGC will be provided.

In Part III, Overarching Issues in Developing a Sustainable Approach to Family Support, we explore issues that provide a connection between our specific practice areas. Two chapters are provided which explore:

- multi-disciplinary working; and
- professional workforce development.

It is argued, in chapter 10, that effective multi-disciplinary work should underpin family support. A theoretical approach is recommended and explored. How this maps onto work with families is explained and argued for.

In chapter 11, the often neglected issue of workforce development is explored. This chapter proposes that the core of family support work has shifted from 'social work' settings to voluntary sector settings, and this has profound implications for the sustainability of family support and for workforce development. The current state of workforce development and a previously unpublished survey undertaken by the authors are presented. A proposed way forward is discussed.

The final chapter provides a critical overview of the material presented throughout the book. It identifies links between the past, present and future of family support and suggests future directions for the development of the family support agenda.

At the end of the book, we provide a resource guide which will help professionals put into practice some of the ideas and challenges provided in the first three parts of the book. These include:

- useful websites;
- family support organizations;
- training packs and practical resources;
- bibliography.

**PART I**

UNDERSTANDING FAMILY SUPPORT

# 1 The Historical, Social and Political Context of Family Support

This chapter explores the historical roots and origins of family support in order to understand the contested definitions, theories and practice of family support in the contemporary policy context. Throughout the book, we will make the argument for family support as a fundamental practice within child welfare, and we will explore the implications for policy makers, researchers and practitioners alike of placing family support at the centre of child welfare policy and practice.

Understanding the historical context is crucial if we are to situate current debates within child welfare and if we are to truly understand continued tensions in the wider realm of child welfare policy and practice. Since the 1970s, high-profile child deaths, subsequent media campaigns, public concern and political controversy have together created a seemingly irresistible move towards a potentially punitive child protection system based upon an emphasis on risk assessment and authoritarian intervention. This varies across the globe and is perhaps more apparent in England, whilst being less so in Scotland, Wales and Northern Ireland. This trend towards risk assessment-based work has contributed to the marginalization of prevention and family support: thus child protection has become increasingly dominant at the cost of more partnership and family support-based practices. This key tension has dominated the literature, and the argument for a rebalancing of family support and child protection has been widely discussed (for example, see Featherstone, White and Morris 2014; Frost and Parton 2009; Parton 1997).

Whilst debates within child welfare about whether to use 'family support', 'early help' or 'early intervention' may seem technical and perhaps obscure, we see them as actually key to wider social issues of concern to us all: debates about social equality, childhood, opportunity and well-being. As Featherstone and colleagues have commented on the influential work of Wilkinson and Pickett:

> A linked insight from their work concerns how inequality within a society quite literally 'gets under the skin' of individuals, leaving them feeling unvalued and inferior. They note the work of the sociologist Thomas Scheff, who has argued that shame is a key social emotion. 'Shame and its opposite, pride, are rooted in the processes through which we internalize how we imagine others see us' . . . Greater inequality heightens our

> anxieties because it increases the importance of social status. We come
> to see social position as a key feature of a person's identity in an unequal
> society.' (Featherstone, Morris and White 2013: 4)

Thus the concerns around family support link to wider concerns about poverty, inequality, identity and well-being. Structural problems, such as poverty and inequality, generate social problems, such as child neglect and child abuse, and are linked to the nature of state intervention in family life. These are the core concerns of family support workers.

In this book, we argue for comprehensive family support for all families rather than, for example, narrow programmatic, time-limited approaches. Family support needs to operate alongside wider-scale economic and social reforms. Thus we maintain that we should not separate debates about family support from those about poverty and inequality. We live in an era of gross inequalities, both within specific societies and more widely between different nation-states. For example, it has been estimated that 30 per cent of children in the United Kingdom live in poverty, compared with other developed European countries such as Norway, where it is 4 per cent (Browne 2012).

Post-global crash public-spending restrictions and benefit reforms in many late capitalist societies have increased trends towards inequality. A major programme of research funded by the Family and Parenting Institute (Browne 2012) analysed the experiences of 'Families in an Age of Austerity'. The research indicates that families with children are 'shouldering a disproportionate burden' of the austerity measures (Browne 2012: 3). The disparity increased in 2014, seeing families with children with children losing 6 per cent of their income, compared to the 2 per cent lost by pensioner households, and also losing more income than working-age households without children (3 per cent), as well as all households (3 per cent) (Browne 2012: 3). In England, it is particularly concerning that the lowest-income families seem to be losing the most through the reforms, thus undermining the intentions of the Child Poverty Act 2010 and its avowed aims of reducing child poverty. In Scotland, Wales and Northern Ireland, there are specific anti-child-poverty programmes which underpin family support policy. For example, the Welsh government is promoting a programme known as 'Tackling Poverty and Promoting Children's Rights'. Child poverty in Northern Ireland is analysed in a report known as *Child Poverty in Northern Ireland* (Child Poverty Alliance 2014). The Scottish approach works towards three outcomes as follows:

- Maximizing household resources – our aim is to reduce income poverty and material deprivation by maximizing financial entitlements and reducing pressure on household budgets among low-income families, as well as by maximizing the potential for parents to increase family incomes through good-quality, sustained employment and by promoting greater financial inclusion and capability. (Pockets)
- Improving children's well-being and life chances – our aim is to break intergenerational cycles of poverty, inequality and deprivation. This requires a focus on tackling the underlying social and economic deter-

minants of poverty and improving the circumstances in which children grow up – recognizing the particular importance of improving children's outcomes in the early years. (Prospects)
- Children from low-income households live in well-designed, sustainable places – our aim is to address area-based factors which currently exacerbate the effects of individual poverty for many families by continuing to improve the physical, social and economic environments in local areas, particularly in those areas of multiple deprivation in which child poverty is more prevalent. (Places)

Whilst this book is aimed specifically at that those professionals involved in child welfare practice, the issues raised here are fundamental to wider debates around problems such as poverty which are central to the well-being and quality of life for all citizens.

> **Point for reflection:** What are the links between poverty, inequality and family support practice?

## Child welfare in history: 1870–1914

It is essential to place contemporary debates about family support in a wider historical context. The origins of child welfare can been found in the nineteenth century, characterized by the *rescuing* and *reclamation* of children predominantly through the heritage of the Poor Law, and were led by emerging philanthropic organizations. Victorian constructions of child welfare practice enabled the practitioner to understand the concepts of risk, danger and child cruelty within failing families which were seen as 'feckless' and 'immoral' (see Gordon 1988). The National Society for the Prevention of Cruelty to Children (NSPCC) acquired predominant responsibility for both preventing and addressing child cruelty. It adopted a largely reforming approach towards parents in contrast to the early 'rescue' approach, favoured by Dr Thomas Barnardo, for example (Frost and Stein 1989). These early practices highlight the fact that child welfare was at the time predominantly in the sphere of philanthropy; the national, state-based interest in children and families emerged in the late nineteenth century, to be consolidated by the Children Act 1908 (Hendrick 2003).

The shift in attitude towards intervention in childhood, exemplified by the foundation of organizations such as the NSPCC, developed after the British industrial revolution, when cities grew rapidly and social processes developed a professional and commercial bourgeoisie. It is estimated that at least five million people were removed from their homes to make way for industrial change (Stedman Jones 1976). The British industrial revolution led to rapidly growing cities and often grim conditions for the new industrial working class. A crucial impact of this was the attempt to control the poor, the 'dangerous' and the 'feckless' by rendering them liable to philanthropic and state intervention (Hendrick 2003).

The influential social historian Harry Hendrick contends that this industrialization and urbanization process led to a situation where 'children were given a new social and political identity as belonging to the nation' (2003: 19) at the end of the nineteenth and the start of the next century. Reforms, such as the Children Act 1908, embodied a wider range of services provision for families, including public access to health and education. These reforms were largely motivated by concerns about the health and well-being of children, who were seen as essential to the future of Britain as an industrial, imperial and military power (Hendrick 2003).

In the late nineteenth century, the exercise of unfettered parental (or more specifically paternal) responsibility had significantly decreased and marked the beginning of tensions between parental and state authority. A shift in attitude had emerged which meant that the welfare of children began to take precedence over parental claims to privacy and authority over their families.

## A brief history of the NSPCC

The NSPCC was founded in the United Kingdom in 1884. Lord Shaftesbury was appointed as president and Reverend Benjamin Waugh and Edward Rudolf as joint honorary secretaries. This came about as a result of a letter from Reverend George Staite published in the *Liverpool Mercury*, highlighting the significant impact of abuse, cruelty and inhumanity on children, underpinned by social deprivation and inequality. The letter called for the formation of a society to prevent cruelty to children and is in retrospect a landmark in the history of child welfare (Frost and Stein 1989). Victorian social attitudes remained clear on the boundaries between public and private lives; however, Staite wrote a letter to Lord Shaftesbury, a leading philanthropist, requesting legislative backing for intervention in abusive families. Although Shaftesbury agreed that the evils of child abuse were 'enormous and 'indisputable', he also stated 'they are of so private, internal and domestic a character as to be beyond the reach of legislation' (quoted in Behlmer 1982: 52). Shaftesbury's response highlights the predominant attitude at the time: that the family home was inviolable and not to be disturbed or intruded upon. This dividing line between the family and the state remains the key tension in child welfare, a divide that family support continually negotiates and brokers.

The social, economic and political climate of the time is crucial to understanding the continued struggle of the NSPCC to bring child abuse into the public domain. The profoundly unequal condition of the United Kingdom created a chasm of wealth disparity, and after living with and witnessing the deprivation of children in his home town of Greenwich, London, Waugh began to draw public and government attention to the social condition of children. Influential observers at the time began to see that the 'poor' needed assistance in aspiring to the domestic model of family life, and that this adverse lifestyle was not only impacting the poor, but also the respectable working class, whose values of responsibility and independence were being undermined (Hendrick 2003: 24).

The initial delivery model of the first SPCC (Society for the Protection of Cruelty to Children) focused on parenting support, rather than prosecution, and sought to keep children within their homes, unlike much of the development of the nineteenth-century practices of child rescue, carried out by Barnardo, for example. The intention was to 'deal directly with the parents and to reform the home rather than punish the culprits' (Behlmer 1982: 55).

Following the initial growth in influence of the NSPCC, the legislative reform of the 1889 Prevention of Cruelty to Children Act demonstrated for the first time that child protection had become a public concern that could generate public and political support.

The Children Act 1908, which applied to the entire United Kingdom, followed and highlighted the shift towards parental responsibility and punishment, strengthening the law to include 'wilful cruelty and negligence'. Cruelty included the failure to provide adequate food, shelter or clothing, or, if parents were unable to do so, then 'failure to take such steps to procure the same to be provided under the Acts relating to the relief of the Poor'. These court powers and responsibilities were largely a result of the NSPCC's drive to ensure and reinforce parental responsibility for the welfare of children (Ferguson 2004: Gordon 1988).

> **Point for reflection:** How does social history influence our present practice?

## Child deaths, 'moral panics' and the displacement of family support

To understand more recent thinking, we move on to explore developments in the last three decades of the twentieth century. The death of Maria Colwell in 1973 (Parton 1985), a child in care placed back with her mother by social workers, triggered a chain of events that fundamentally changed the role of children's services with families. Maria Colwell was one of nine children and had been in foster care for five years with her aunt, before being returned, aged six years eight months, to live her mother and stepfather. Maria herself communicated opposing returning home, and upon visits had been observed to show signs of trauma. Maria's feelings were marginalized and, in the last nine months of her short life, more than thirty complaints were made about her treatment at the hands of her mother and stepfather. Various visits were made by social workers, yet on 6 January 1973, approximately two weeks before she was to be seven years old, Maria was murdered, 'battered' to death by her stepfather (Parton 1985).

Following Maria's death, Parton claims that the subsequent events created a 'moral panic', defined by sociologist Stanley Cohen as 'a condition or episode [that] emerges to become defined as a threat to societal values and interests' (Cohen 2005: 9; see also Parton 1985). The inquiry that followed was published in 1975 and challenged professional accountability of social workers and their failure to act. Maria's death attracted high-profile media and political attention which contributed to the reform of child welfare practice in a direction that was to influence future policy for decades to come. A string of other high-profile child deaths during the rest of the twentieth century compounded the public and political view that social workers were 'failing to keep children safe' (Jeffrey 2003: 22).

The period prior to Maria's death was seen by some as a 'golden age' of family support and prevention in social work (Corby 2006). An era of prevention was characterized by high staff morale and a sense of shared vision and cohesion. Childcare departments had wide-scale societal support, having been established by a collectivist welfare ideology that found its expression in the formation of key elements of the welfare state following the end of the Second World War (Corby 2006).

The Colwell inquiry influenced childcare policy and in the period between 1974 and 1976 a number of new procedures were outlined in government policy documents. The main elements were the introduction of case conferences, area review committees and child abuse registers for those 'at risk' (Parton 1985), which have become the core of contemporary child protection practice. The focus of social work shifted and became preoccupied with how to recognize the signs of child abuse and the investigation and assessment of child abuse at the expense of a previously more holistic family-based approach. Social workers were required to move away from working with parents to support the welfare of children to providing children with protection from their parents and families (Corby 2006). Therefore, family support had started to become sidelined, differentiated and less significant in the face of a more zealous discovery, pursuit and risk assessment of child abuse. This tension continued following a string of other child deaths and subsequent childcare policy shifts: these included high-profile inquiries into deaths such as those in the 1980s of Jasmine Beckford, Kimberly Carlisle and Tyra Henry through to the deaths of children such as Victoria Climbié and Peter Connelly in the 2000s (Frost and Parton 2009).

## Understanding the impact of child deaths

Ferguson (2004), in his fascinating work drawing on social history and social theory, raises a key question: why is it that the death of a child causes such public outcry in contemporary western societies? Ferguson contrasts current 'moral panics' with the nineteenth-century deaths of children in child protection cases which were 'of routine occurrence and not the subject of public outcry at all' (2004: 9) and where knowledge of child death was actually perceived to be the sign of an effective child protection system. There is powerful statistical evidence that children in the current context of the child protection system have never been safer; thus Ferguson believes that there is a 'central paradox of contemporary concern' (2004: 9) that fixates on child deaths during a time when the system has never been more effective.

The focus on the assessment of risk and on perceived failings within the child protection system provides an essential context for the family support argument. Because attention is drawn to the extraordinary and rare examples of child death, this contributes to fewer resources, less time and reduced human resources being invested in a holistic, preventative and, arguably, economically efficient practice of family support. Thus there is a chasm between the messages from family support research (see chapter 3) and those from serious case reviews and other reports relating to individual child deaths.

In summary, child welfare services in much of the 'late capitalist' world have moved significantly towards a bureaucratic risk-averse culture and away from approaches based on support, partnership and prevention. In the overpowering and dominant response to child deaths, welfare states are increasingly seeking bureaucratic risk-assessment approaches which have potentially led to a crisis in the child welfare system.

> **Point for reflection:** Media and political child deaths have a significant impact on British child welfare practice. Does this have a negative impact on developing family support policy and practice?

## The Children Act 1989

The Children Act of 1989 is perhaps the key to understanding recent shifts in family support policy and issues around the implementation and operationalization of Section 17 of the Act. Drawing on the background of the Cleveland crisis (Frost and Stein 1989) and a number of child death inquiries, the Children Act 1989 was a central piece of legislation and became fundamental to the debate around rebalancing child welfare and child protection.

Section 17 of the Act placed a general duty on local authorities 'to safeguard and promote the welfare of children in their area who were in need, and subject to that duty, to promote the upbringing of such children by their families'. This triggered the use of family support as a key concept, championed by the senior civil servant, Rupert Hughes. Crucially for family support services, the emphasis of Section 17 was on the local authority's statutory duty to provide support for children and families (under Part III of the Children Act 1989). This reinforced family support work and the coordination of work with agencies that were carrying out supportive and preventative work. One of the novel characteristics of this piece of legislation was its explicit underpinning by a set of explicitly stated values (Gibbons 1992). Within the publication *Principles and Practice in Guidance and Regulations* (Department of Health 1989) are a number of key principles crucial to understanding the current discourse around early help, including partnership with parents, the importance of birth families and the centrality of the views of the child (Gibbons 1992: 160).

However, Parton (1991), writing as the Act was being implemented, predicted that Part V and Section 47 (local authorities' duty to investigate 'significant harm') of the Act would dominate the discourses of children's services in the future, and that concerns around thresholds for significant harm would become the main agenda.

These concerns were evidently realized, and, in Parton's follow-up work some years later (1997), he explains the reasons behind his judgements, utilizing two main arguments. His first argument is that the legislative changes had been influenced by high-profile child abuse inquiries and introduced into a 'hostile climate' which is supported and further explored by Frost (1992). Secondly, Parton states that the Children Act 1989 is insignificant when compared to the context of the changes to the economy, increases in social inequality and changes in local government funding which have more direct and indirect impact on day-to-day child policy and practice (Parton 1997). Parton's second argument is articulated as follows: 'not only are the family support aspirations and sections of the Act being implemented partially and not prioritized, but the child protection system is overloaded and not coping with increased demands made of it' (Parton 1997: 3). This child protection focus in turn jeopardizes the effective operation of the family support system.

The debate and tension between family support and child protection has generated a large number of responses in numerous policy documents and within the academic literature addressing the question: how do we develop practice in accordance with the original intentions of the Children Act 1989? (see, for example, Aldgate, Tunstill and McBeath 1994; Department of Health 1991; Home Office 1998; Munro 2004, 2011a, 2011b; Packman and Jordan 1991; Parton 1997). Amongst the most influential significant earlier contributions were the publications *Child Protection: Messages from Research* (Department of Health 1995) and the Audit Commission report, *Seen but Not Heard: Coordinating Community Child Health and Social Services for Children in Need* (1994). Both these publications suggested that the central aims of the Children Act 1989 around the support of families were not being effectively implemented.

*Child Protection: Messages from Research* (Department of Health 1995) argues the case for viewing the child protection system in a wider context in that incidents of harm should not be viewed in isolation from a holistic view of the child's story. This debate permeates contemporary discourse and demonstrates that, whilst there have been significant differences and changes, the core issues of the under-resourced and underemphasized Section 17 of the Children Act, 1989, remain.

Examining the nature of the debate around child protection and family support shows that shifts take place in a cyclical manner, continually revisiting the relationship between the child, the family and the state (Frost 2011). These evolving debates in social policy arguably do not follow a linear pattern but a rotary one, which continues to redefine, theorize and debate the same issues continually (Rein 1983). Childcare social policy is therefore informed largely by a changing political climate and economic backdrop, and the shifting hegemonic discourse of the time.

Thus far, we have reviewed some of the relevant literature which highlights that the origins of family support lie in the Victorian history of child welfare. Notions derived from the Poor Law, including the 'deserving/ undeserving poor' dichotomy, remain present in the current discourse of family support. A discourse around an individualistic blame model through apparent failures in parenting, and cycles of societal ills illustrated by delinquent youth, generates perceived necessary, yet undesirable, state intervention (Parton 1985, Field 2010). This in turn generates a tension between family support and child protection which is explored in much of this book.

## Defining our terms

As this book emphasizes throughout, the terms 'prevention', 'family support', 'early help' and 'early intervention' are used in a variety of ways within literature, policy and practice, demonstrating that there are no fixed definitions or understandings, thus highlighting the significant divergence in theory, practice and service delivery models. In the remainder of this chapter, we explore definition and deployment of these terms. We argue that family support is the most resilient and sustainable of these concepts and, in terms of values and ethics, the most acceptable. One intellectually helpful framework for exploring these issues is that originally devised by Pauline Hardiker and colleagues: known as the 'Hardiker Model' (see Figure 1.1), we will use this to explore some of the underpinning issues and controversies.

The Hardiker Model provides an analytical framework that allows us to

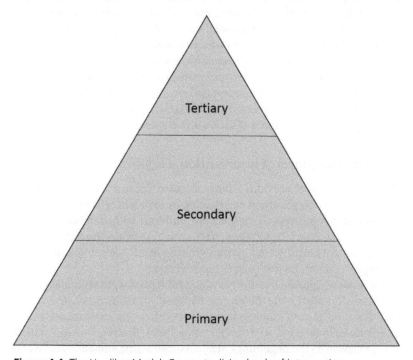

**Figure 1.1** The Hardiker Model: Conceptualizing levels of intervention

demonstrate different levels of need and how policy and practice can be developed utilizing this model. The Hardiker Model can assist practitioners within children's services to explore the roots of what has now become widely identified as *thresholds of intervention*, and it can also be used for planning and delivering family support services. Originally, the model was developed within a study of four proposed models of welfare: the residual model, the institutional model, the developmental model and the radical conflict model of welfare (Hardiker, Exton and Barker 1991a). These crucial political and social contexts were used as background to examine the preventative activity with relation to levels of intervention: primary, secondary and tertiary (Hardiker, Exton and Barker 1989). These terms have been adapted but originate from medical model concepts involving levels which were utilized to create ameliorative goals for early intervention practice within mental and public health. As there was some deliberation over the definitions of secondary and tertiary prevention, a fourth dimension was later added and expanded to add a fourth, or quaternary, level of intervention.

## The primary level of intervention

The primary level is widely understood as the 'universal' level underpinning all stages. At the primary level, services such as sufficient housing, health, income and education are necessary to meet an individual's needs and should be universally accessed accordingly. In Northern Ireland, UNOCINI (Understanding the Needs of Children in Northern Ireland) published guidance on what they developed as a 'thresholds-of-need model', in which primary prevention is usefully applied as follows: 'The majority of children and families in Northern Ireland whose needs are being met. They utilize universal services and community resources as required' (2011: 1).

Universal services are widely understood as necessary for all children and families and are generally accepted as a part of family life. They can be accessed widely without any element of stigma: open access to a local playground provides an example of such a universal service.

## The secondary level of intervention

The secondary level provides a more targeted approach to service provision. It addresses highlighted needs, often by means of referral for children and young people usually defined as 'children with additional needs' (Brandon et al. 2008). This approach is normally provided through a voluntary agreement and often incorporates the use of third-sector organizations in the provision of services such as home visiting.

There is a suggestion that the transition from primary to secondary levels of prevention marks the difference between an unknown client/family and the allocation of client status and therefore the early stages of the intervention of targeted services (Richards 1987). This relationship in itself can be viewed as the beginnings of stigmatized status and an invasive and potentially detrimental process. Some believe that this can no longer be considered 'prevention' although, as highlighted by Hardiker et al. (1991a), a key goal of social intervention, such as family support, is to restore individuals to more autonomy and help them to retain social links offered at the primary intervention level. Therefore, a crucial objective is to prevent the necessity of increasingly intrusive interventions (Hardiker et al. 1991a: 349). Consequently, the secondary level moves into case work: the objectives may be similar to those at the primary level but the work focus moves from wider structures of networks and communities to identified individuals and families: records and case files are often kept as part of this process.

## The tertiary level of intervention

The third level is a more complex level of work, usually defined as involving some sort of child protection or safeguarding activity for 'children with complex needs' (Brandon et al. 2008). These are more intensive approaches and intervention measures enacted within a statutory framework because risk and vulnerability are high (Hardiker et al. 1991a). This work is carried out with increasingly narrow and specified objectives, such as protecting a child from significant harm. The emphasis is drawn from legislation within the Children Act 1989 and the investigatory procedures under Section 47. At this level, there is an increased emphasis on procedure, enforcement and surveillance: Jeffrey claims that 'social workers have tended to focus their efforts, more or less exclusively, on child protection work and on children seen to be at risk of significant harm' (2003: 34).

## The quaternary level of intervention

The fourth level, added later to the model, can be understood as the rehabilitation of children and young people: this may be a therapeutic intervention or the return home of children from state care, for example. This level of intervention emphasizes the developments that can be made at this stage, such as the importance of maintaining links with families and reversing damage to children through the possible negative outcomes of a care placement: it can address issues of self-esteem, separation, loss and threats to identity (Hardiker et al. 1991a).

The main difference at this level of work is it should 'minimise the damage that may arise as a result of entry into care' (Hardiker et al. 1991a: 350). The definition is broad and possibly outdated as there are now more positive approaches and discourses in regard to the care system, in particular, a challenge to rethink residential care as a more creative and positive intervention (see Smith 2009). Although the state care system has some serious challenges and shortfalls to address, at the fourth level professionals are expected to make decisions based upon the original ideals of rehabilitating a child in a new environment whilst understanding the impact of such choices.

## Some limitations of the Hardiker Model

The Hardiker Model has been profoundly influential in terms of understanding family support, and indeed children's services, more widely: we will utilize this approach throughout this book to inform our study. However, there are, almost inevitably, shortcomings to the model. The Hardiker Model is not exhaustive and cannot incorporate all outcomes, needs, concerns, risk factors or services that could potentially be present. Additional conceptual approaches need to be applied in order to develop and mobilize family support approaches more effectively. The context in which the model was first created is also crucial to understanding, as its original format was a two-dimensional table incorporating models of welfare where the term 'prevention' was used with clear objectives and was understood in relation to the value systems it underpins (Hardiker et al. 1991a: 2). The term 'prevention' has sometimes been used negatively as a reaction to something that is already happening, whereas the family support approach is to incorporate a more proactive attitude with families and to promote the development and delivery of services from the outset as we argue in our definition of family support. Family support is crucially a more proactive approach than the reactive idea of prevention.

Whilst the development of the original Hardiker Model into a simplified version (Figure 1.1) is easier to contextualize and apply, the Hardiker Model has now become a *thresholds of needs model*, creating a problematic image of professional rationing and gatekeeping. Furthermore, Table 1.1 represents the modern and possibly more realistic distribution of priorities in service delivery, indicating that children's services are more or less focused exclusively on tertiary and quaternary levels, i.e. on child protection services and the state care system (as described in Frost and Parton 2009).

**Table 1.1** Developing levels of family support

|  | Residual | Institutional | Developmental | Radical |
|---|---|---|---|---|
| **Primary** | Not applicable | Universal children's centres | Parenting education | Universal, free child care |
| **Secondary** | Assessment | Drop-in advice centres | Service-users' support groups | Home visits for all those requiring them |
| **Tertiary** | Assessment | Domestic violence support centres | Family group conferences | Campaigns against male violence |
| **Quaternary** | Reunification | Residential parent and baby homes | Re-parenting classes | Intensive home support |

Family support service delivery can operate at all four levels, as Table 1.1 illustrates. Here, services have been classified using the Hardiker four levels, 'residual', 'institutional', 'developmental' or 'radical', thus giving a grid of service development (see Frost and Dolan 2012 for a discussion of Gilligan's work). The emphasis on the universal and secondary levels has possibly reduced during recent years as service delivery has focused more on risk and crisis management, creating by default a diminishing and displaced family support service, thus moving towards the tertiary and quaternary levels.

Whilst these models are conceptual, as this book will claim, the changes in policy and practice over time illustrate that these shifts have a real impact, creating a profound challenge for children's services which will potentially have a negative impact on families that require differentiated levels of support.

Having explored 'support', we now move on to discuss how the term 'family' is deployed.

## How can we understand 'the family'?

Attempting to define 'family' is complex and contested, as there are many variations in the structure and components of family and family life. The concept of family in contemporary societies, where 'family' and households include a range of different people and varying roles, demonstrates a contrasting range of lived experiences for individuals and households.

The term 'family' is therefore a highly contested one and debates around these issues often have a high political profile. The following examples highlight contrasting views and perspectives on how modern people arrange their caring and emotional lives. Patricia Morgan (1995) is a long-standing champion of 'traditional family life' and has stated that this is in decline, leading to unwelcome changes with potentially preventable negative consequences. She argues from a conservative perspective as follows: 'While the effects of family breakdown are already apparent, acceptance of the end of marriage and decline of the family is premature. The first step towards recovery is to stop describing social changes as though they were inevitable' (Morgan 1995: 82).

In contrast, the CAVA (Cares, Values and the Future of Welfare) research project, as outlined by Fiona Williams (2004), defines family practices as fluid and changing, and not as a fixed social institution. For Williams, family becomes how we *practise* family, rather than a predefined notion of what family is: 'It registers the ways in which our networks of affection are not simply given by virtue of blood and marriage but are negotiated and shaped by us over time and place' (2004: 17).

We can conclude from these two contrasting approaches that there is a significant divergence in what 'family' constitutes and how the consequence of social change should be understood and evaluated. One issue that is clear from examining the academic perspectives on what constitutes family is that family life has changed, the relationships between families have changed, and the societal perception of family life has changed. In summary, this change has moved away from a nuclear family model, whereby men, women and children had predefined, fixed and accepted gender roles within a family unit, to a more gender-interchangeable, fluid and increasingly negotiated sphere of family and household life (Williams 2004). The increasing significant diminished authority of religious institutions, the decline of deference and informal social control over family life and practice has meant that family life is constantly changing and fluid. Perhaps the starkest example across much of the western world is that homosexual couples are now often able to marry, according them the same rights as heterosexual couples, which is undoubtedly creating further shifts in family practices, perspectives and life.

## What is family support?

Although definitions of family may vary, as we have seen, what is clear is that families, in all their diverse forms, lie at the heart of our social life, valued as necessary trajectories in fulfilled, meaningful and connected lives. However, as we have already discussed, there is much confusion about exactly what 'family support' means, and also about which remit family support services are working to. Throughout the literature, subtle differences in definitions illustrate the growing problem of identity around family support policy and practice. A basic definition, which is often quoted, is that provided by the Audit Commission: 'Any activity or facility provided either by statutory agencies or by community groups or individuals, aimed at providing advice and support to parents to help them in bringing up their children' (1994: 1).

Family support has become a phrase that is used so often and in varying capacities that it has lost its meaning and become difficult to define (Penn and Gough 2002). As a result, the term has been used to pioneer various interventions and targeting of services, influencing various debates about what we understand to be effective targeting of groups and timely intervention.

Frost (2003) describes family support as a 'slippery concept', while Featherstone (2004) uses the term 'empty category' when discussing family support. Family support can comprise a number of meanings and definitions and this highlights the importance of 'unpacking' the spaces that it occupies (Featherstone 2004). Whatever way family support is understood and deployed, it is clear that it must be positioned within the complex triangular interactions between child, family and state (see Frost 2011).

Statham (2000) highlights the importance of understanding family support through its characteristics, pointing out that it can be delivered at any level of intervention using the Hardiker Model. Other researchers, including Hearn, provide similar definitions: 'Family support is about the creation of and enhancement, with and for families in need, of locally based or accessible activities, facilities and networks, the use of which have outcomes such as alleviated stress, increased self-esteem, promoted parental/carer/family competence and behaviour and increased parental/carer capacity to nurture and protect children' (Hearn 1995: 2).

As well as understanding some of the characteristics of family support, a key component of its definition is the *method* by which the services are delivered. Fundamentally, as we have seen, the style of working predominantly promotes partnership, empowerment, relationship-based practice and the interpersonal relationships between the service providers and the families, thus ensuring crucially that the *process* and not the *product* is emphasized.

The imbalance between child protection and family support is not surprising, given the variety of perceptions of what family support means in practice. A review of the literature and official reports that have developed from an attempt to understand how Section 17 is carried out in practice, and how it is associated with wider childcare policy, illustrates the extent of the various interpretations of family support. The family support literature borders on other policy and practice issues, including, for example:

- the prevention of abuse (Featherstone, White and Morris 2014);
- community care delivery and empowerment (Frost, Lloyd and Jeffery 2003);
- service delivery to children in need (Tunstill 1995);
- supporting parents with children who have learning disabilities or are otherwise disabled (Bailey, Raspa and Fox 2012);
- improved parenting support (Pugh, De'Ath and Smith 1994; Utting 1995);
- targeted delivery to child abuse cases (Thoburn, Wilding and Watson. 2000);
- home-visiting support through voluntary engagement with parents (Frost et al. 1996; Oakley, Rajan and Turner 1998);
- integrated service delivery in universal services. (Glass 1999, 2006)

Examining the development of family support from a historical perspective helps to demonstrate the shift from the previous directions in childcare policy and can assist in unpacking misconceptions as to what family support means currently in policy and practice. This also highlights the need for government and service providers to develop a working definition within a conceptual framework which is inclusive of areas of need and varying service approaches to these (Pinkerton, Dolan and Canavan 2004). Such a statement has been provided, for example, by the government of the Republic of Ireland in 2000 in the 'National Children's Strategy: Our Children – Their Lives', where a family support orientation is evident. There is a danger of minimal and disjointed aspects of policy approaches being implemented, creating difficulty in both evaluation and evidence of cost effectiveness in family support services (as brilliantly established by Rutter 2006).

Family support needs to be understood in the context of the following three approaches: within a conceptual policy framework, within an economic and political context, and through the characteristics of service delivery. All three of these areas will be explored in various ways through-out this book, thus forming a holistic perspective.

> **Point for reflection:** Is it a significant problem that there is no single, uni-versally accepted definition of family support?

## Family support: why and how?

First, why do we think the term 'family support' is helpful? We argue that language really matters, constructing legitimate versions of the world and obscuring or negating others. Thus we recognize some of the dangers of using the term 'family' in the context of the diversity of forms and ways of living family life. Politically, there is an important critique to be made of exclusive notions of family which rest upon moralizing and/or authoritar-ian approaches to those seen as 'deviant' or failing. Indeed, the capture of the term 'family' is recognized as it speaks to deeply rooted longings and reflects everyday personal practices. The language of family emphasizes connectedness and relationships, unlike, as explored above, a language of child protection that situates the individual and, indeed often, idealized child separately from their families (Featherstone, White and Morris 2014).

## Early intervention

Early intervention has become an increasingly central concept during the last decade. There has been a plethora of official documents, think-tank reports and research studies arguing the case for prevention through early intervention within child welfare policy. As a result, the terms 'early intervention' and 'early help' have to a degree displaced the use of 'family support'.

Reports that emphasize 'early intervention' as a key concept include the following:

- *Grasping the Nettle: Early Intervention for Children, Families and Communities* (Centre 4 Excellence and Outcomes 2010b);
- *The Foundation Years: Preventing Poor Children Becoming Poor Adults* (Field 2010);
- *Early Intervention: The Next Steps* (Allen 2011);
- *Early Intervention: Good Parents, Great Kids, Better Citizens* (Allen and Duncan Smith 2008);
- *Deprivation and Risk: The Case for Early Intervention* (Action for Children 2010);
- *The Early Years: Foundations for Life, Health and Learning* (Tickell 2011).

Consistent key themes emerge from these documents. The Centre for Social Justice Report *Making Sense of Early Intervention* (Centre for Social Justice 2011) suggests that an effective framework based upon these reports would contain the following six elements:

1.   A commitment to prevention
2.   Priority focus on the early years
3.   Continuing early intervention in later years
4.   A multi-agency systems approach
5.   High quality of work force
6.   Investment in programmes that work (Centre for Social Justice 2011)

It is clear that the focus on 'early intervention' is moving increasingly centre-stage in child welfare policy. In England, at least, there seems to be an official consensus that intervening earlier to prevent problems, rather than costly reactive responses to developed and ingrained problems is an approach 'with whom few would disagree' (Deacon 2011). Similar debates are taking place in Scotland, Wales and Northern Ireland. However, as we have seen, there is considerable confusion within this debate around language, definitions, policy and fundamentally what services should be provided and by whom.

The notion of dealing with problems early to improve social and economic outcomes appeals to common sense, which is one reason why the arguments in favour of early intervention have gained wide-scale, cross-party enthusiasm and support. It is also often grounded in the emphasis on research findings from neuroscience which we discuss in chapter 3.

Although there is a certain consistency in the emerging themes in the reports listed above, there is inconsistency in defining prevention, early intervention and early help. Differences in emphasis and language have created subtle variations in the approach to the concept as illustrated by the following two definitions of early intervention:

- the general approaches and the specific policies and programmes, which help to give children age 0–3 the social and emotional bedrock they need to become the good parents of tomorrow (Allen 2011: xi);
- intervening early and as soon as possible to tackle problems emerging for children, young people and their families or with a population most at risk of developing problems. (Centre 4 Excellence and Outcomes 2010a: 4).

The key difference between these two definitions is how wide or small the net is cast for early intervention. Essentially, the Allen report focuses, more or less exclusively, on the early years, predominantly the critical age bracket of 0–3 years. This age bracket has developed from the recent fixation of neuroscience with early brain development as discussed in chapter 3. This has driven a seemingly irresistible agenda to prevent the loss of vital social and emotional cognitive functioning which, if problems are not confronted early enough, can be lost for ever, it is claimed, once the clock strikes midnight on a child's third birthday. It follows that, whilst a focus on the early years is vital, it is not itself adequate, and further emphasis must be put on the entire span of a child's or young person's life, and on the timing to prevent further problems arising. Family support describes a wider age range of support, the 'early' being implicit in both intervention and support.

Early intervention essentially derives from the notion that if you inter-vene 'early enough' (particularly in the pre-school age of a child), you are stopping society's bedrock from crumbling, averting social ills and, as a linear consequence, avoiding further social problems, thus preventing a domino effect. The range of social problems which can be prevented are described in the Allen report (2011) as:

- crime (especially violent crime);
- poor examination results;
- higher rates of teenage pregnancy;
- lower rates of employment;
- higher rates of depression and suicide;
- substance misuse. (Allen 2011: 4)

As with family support, this inconsistent use of language and its inter-pretation, along with the lack of a strict universal definition, is key to understanding early intervention in the context of current policy initiatives. The terms are used broadly, 'interchangeably and imprecisely' (Plimmer and Van Poortvliet 2012: 9) to refer to the pre-empting of social problems by focusing on the causes of the issues, as opposed to purely managing the consequences.

The following quote, used by Iain Duncan Smith, later a Cabinet member in the 2010–2015 British coalition government, in one of the key reports, *Early Intervention: Good Parents, Great Kids, Better Citizens* (Allen and Duncan Smith 2008), demonstrates the emphasis on the 'inevitable' occur-rence of social problems: 'The approach we are recommending aims for prevention by early intervention: prevention of ill-preparedness for school and other learning environments; prevention of the adoption of the violent behaviour that makes toddlers anti-social school children unmanageable and ends up with young people languishing in prison' (Allen and Duncan Smith 2008: 24).

Notably in this definition, early intervention and prevention are com-bined to end the problem of 'anti-social' and 'unmanageable' children who 'perpetuate the cycle of dysfunction' (Allen and Duncan Smith 2008: 24). Use of this language further compounds the worrying trend in contempo-rary discussion to apportion blame rather than examine social causation and proposes simplified solutions to 'wicked' social problems.

The use of language around prevention and early intervention, accord-ing to the Dartington Social Research Unit (2004), highlights that 'one person's prevention is another person's intervention. There is much confu-sion over the term, and no single definition can be counted on as definitive' (2004: 18). A broad distinction is recognized by some between 'prevention', intervening before an issue arises, and 'early intervention', reacting to an already established problem in its early stages (Little 1999). This lack of clarity about the characteristics of preventative services has led to a diverse range of these being provided by the statutory, voluntary and community sectors, resulting in a lack of consistency, overlap and worrying gaps in provision for the most marginalized.

As discussed in chapter 2, early intervention is not only about the way in which it is defined in relation to the critical stages of a child's life, but it must also be understood within the complete picture of recommended service delivery. The issue of defining the bracket of children who qualify for an early intervention goes hand in hand with the narrow silo-natured and programme-led approach to service delivery, as outlined in chapter 2, and signifies the reductionist and product-driven incentives of the early intervention agenda.

## Early help definition

'Early help' can be understood as the most recent development of a term to describe the contemporary approach to supporting children and families: arguably, it sits somewhere between family support and early intervention. The Munro (2011b) report was commissioned by the 2010–2015 coalition government to review the child protection system. Munro's *Review* was unusual in that it was not instigated by an inquiry into a child death or as a reactive response to a serious incident. The review is underpinned by theory, informed by research and includes data from the consultation of 250 children, young people and parents (Munro 2011b). The emergence of the Munro report and its distinct distancing from the use of the term 'early intervention' through its replacement with the term 'early help' opened up a new domain in the power of language: 'The review uses the term "help" rather than the more commonly used term "intervention" in describing professional services because "help" carries a stronger connotation of working with families and supporting their aims and efforts to change' (Munro 2011a: 21).

This specific differentiation made here between the two terms, 'help' and 'intervention', highlights the subtle nature of language, its connotations and the importance of terminology. Munro develops this further by recognizing the problem in defining her term: '"Early help" is an ambiguous term, referring both to help in the early years of a child or young person's life and early in the emergence of a problem at any stage in their lives' (Munro 2011b: 69)

With the clarification outlined here, early help already addresses the issues early intervention could not resolve. In encompassing the early years and the early stages of a problem, 'early help' as a term has far more positive and progressive thematic connotations when compared to the narrower focus of early intervention.

## Why early help?

The Munro report identifies three principal arguments for endorsing early help:

- the moral imperative to minimize suffering;
- the prevention of damage rather than its reversal;
- cost effectiveness. (Munro 2011b)

There is an acknowledgement that first and foremost of these characteristics is the 'moral imperative' to minimize suffering, rather than the previous focus on preventing the further entrenchment of problems. Munro (2011b) clarifies that, throughout the report, early help encompasses the wide spectrum of prevention throughout childhood, and not just the early years. In her interim report *The Munro Review of Child Protection Interim Report* (2011a), Munro discusses the importance in recognizing different levels of need and, through the use of the Hardiker Model, the 'merits of [a] primary and secondary preventative service' (Munro 2011a: 94). Munro clarifies that the emphasis of the report, which is on 'children who are suffering or likely to suffer significant harm as a result of maltreatment' (2011a: 21), is necessary when analysing the child protection system. In contrast to many of the reports mentioned above, Munro's (2011b) recommendations are refreshing in their endeavour to examine and discuss the child protection system critically: a system which is, as she correctly conceptualizes, 'complex'.

## Key themes emerging from Munro

In her interim report, Munro outlines key themes in relation to 'getting help early' and explains the terminology used. It contains a 'considerable body of evidence' to show that 'intervening early can save costly interventions' (Munro 2011a: 22). As well as her endorsement of Allen's (2011) work on evidence-based programmes, she also acknowledges that 'many approaches already exist', highlighting initiatives such as Sure Start and Home-Start which reinforce the importance of the community and voluntary sector and place engagement with families at their centre (Munro 2011a: 22), as discussed further throughout this book.

A fundamental shift from previous perspectives on early intervention and targeted support to early help is marked by the notion and recommendation that families receive help when needs are identified, rather than intervention after a problem arises. Munro (2011b) recommends that, in order to achieve this, local authorities need to outline packages of help available to families, so that the needs are actually met and not just assessed.

## Relationships and partnership

Family engagement and partnership are fundamental to differentiating between early intervention and early help. It is one of the crucial factors in distinguishing between an intervention with a family or child, or support provided for a family or child – whether it is intervention or help. Evidence shows that partnership with families is instrumental in strengthening positive outcomes for children (Department of Health 1995; Macmillan et al. 2009; Munro 2011a). The strength-based approach supports children by 'motivating and empowering families to recognize their own needs, strengths, and resources and to take an active role in working toward change' (Steib 2004). Munro (2011a) also recognizes that, although effective engagement with families should always be a priority, 'there are also families whose parenting raises serious concern, and it may be necessary to take a more coercive approach' (Munro 2011a: 21).

Relationships and the quality of direct work are characteristically imperative in the Munro (2011b) report and the early help agenda, and are discussed further in our chapter on relationship-based work. There is recognition that it is as important to examine how things are being done as it is to study what is being done. Relationship-based practice, engagement with families and direct work are the components of the Munro report which proposes a new way of addressing social work, rather than the contemporary focus on procedures, risk, protocol, assessment and gathering data.

Although family support approaches were to the origins of social work (Corby 2006), currently these skills may be viewed as secondary to risk assessment. Throughout the Munro report (2011b), early help seeks to rebalance the role of the relationships between the child, the family and the professional. Recommendations for removing obstacles to these, such as designated timescales and other prescriptive elements of government guidance, sought to rebalance trust in the frontline professional with the autonomy of social workers. This was an attempt to reinforce the human process of child protection, and move away from practice based in enforcement, surveillance and assessment.

## Resources: issues and challenges

It is arguable that social work policy and practice have become increasingly preoccupied with the tertiary and quaternary levels of the Hardiker Model. As discussed, the allocation of resources in children's social care departments can be considered unbalanced, with a large emphasis on crisis-level intervention (tertiary and quaternary) and very little focus on and resources for primary and secondary levels. Rebalancing child protection work and family support has been discussed for many decades. Parton (1997) argues that the focus on risk and child protection has led to resources being allocated away from primary and secondary prevention, a process which underplays inequality as the root cause of child abuse and neglect. Furthermore, the language of 'need' is an ambiguous one when placed within the institutional model of welfare, that 'this restricted definition of support for families and children in need constitutes a new ideology of residualism and this will continue to provide a challenge for good practices in child care' (Hardiker, Exton and Barker 1991b: 357) The challenge remains that, whilst scarce resources are easier to obtain for children on child protection plans, for example, diverting children away from this system using the Hardiker Model and thresholds of need can only succeed if similar resources are available at other levels for family support services.

## Conclusion

This chapter has discussed the conceptual confusions in the field of family support. As well as the need for clearer definitions of family support, early intervention and early help, there is also a responsibility to provide more positive language that promotes resilience rather than merely advocates preventing harm. We also need to develop a discourse that mobilizes the support of informal networks to supplement that provided by professionals.

The Centre for Social Justice recommends that, '[r]ather than the "silo working" of early intervention which often means children and families do not get the bespoke and co-ordinated help they need which can be exacerbated by an overly programmatic approach, we need [an] all-encompassing and pervasive early intervention culture' (2011: 13).

The holistic culture discussed here can be linked to a significant policy document: Professor Eileen Munro's review of child protection (2011b). This review sought to radically shift the silo-natured, bureaucratic perspective into a more relationship-based, holistic culture and decisively replaced the much used 'early intervention' concept with the term 'early help', an approach that family support sits much more comfortably within. This signifies the recognition that a working style and relationship with the child and family is more important than bureaucracy, outcome measures and audit trails.

*Exercise*

Think about a family support project you have worked for or that you have worked with. Using the Hardiker Model described above (pp. 17–21), how would you classify the practice of the organization, using the four levels? Consider how appropriate this is. Could a case be made for moving up or down the levels?

*Discussion*

The Hardiker Model is often used for understanding family support. It is useful for planning services, evaluation and training staff to operate at the different levels. See Table II.1 (p. 55) to illustrate how this can be undertaken.

## Selected further reading

Featherstone, B., White, S. and Morris, K. (2014) *Re-inventing Child Protection*. Bristol: Policy Press. An influential book which explores alternatives to the current focus on safeguarding and a system led by political and media responses to high-profile child deaths.

Ferguson, H. (2004) *Protecting Children in Time*. Basingstoke: Palgrave Macmillan. Another excellent history book, making effective use of social theory and social history to explore early child protection practice.

Gordon, L. (1988) *Heroes of their Own Lives*. London: Virago. Perhaps the best book ever written about the history of child abuse: exploring the roots of child protection practice in the United States at the end of the nineteenth century.

# 2 The Contemporary Policy Context of Family Support: Conceptualizing Family Support

In the field of family support, there is a conceptual battle taking place. As we have seen in chapter 1, the attentive reader of the policy, practice and research literature will find the following terms deployed:

- prevention;
- family support;
- early intervention;
- early help.

Often, such conceptual debates are referred to as 'academic' in the sense that they are not immediately relevant to policy and practice. Here, we demonstrate that these debates really do matter and are far from 'academic': the way that we conceptualize practice has a real impact on how workers practise day to day. In order to understand these issues, we explore policy debates and how the conceptual debate is helping to shape and steer policy and practice.

## Allen and Munro: early intervention or early help?

In the United Kingdom, the election of the coalition government in 2010 signalled a new and emergent interest in 'early intervention'. Evidence of this emerging interest can be seen in the government's commissioning of four major reports relevant to child welfare (see Allen 2011; Field 2010; Munro 2011b; Tickell 2011). A key theme that connected these reports was the concept of 'early intervention'. We will compare and contrast the two reports most relevant to our concerns in this book, the Allen and Munro reports, in terms of how they utilize early help and early intervention.

When comparing the Munro report (2011b) and the review by Graham Allen (2011), it is clear that the language, typologies and concepts used contrast with each other significantly. During 2010–2015, the coalition government showed a significant interest in intervening in the lives of children and young people. The Allen report has had a significant impact on commissioning (Godar 2013) and on the field of research, as we shall see in chapter 3. The recommendations from the Munro report (2011b) have had an impact on child protection practice because the coalition approved most of them (Department for Education 2011), and Professor Munro has since played a significant role in the regime of inspection administered by Ofsted (The Office for Standards in Education, Children's Services and Skills).

Policy discussions relevant to child welfare, child protection and early intervention often occur together in these reports (Centre for Social Justice 2011) in attempts to understand the developments in children's services. However, it is clear that there are significant differences, even contradictions, between the reports which have potentially profound implications for the future of children and childhood.

Whilst the two reports have much in common, the way that language is used and the mobilization of concepts in the reports also demonstrate significant differences. The most important difference is the use of the terms 'early intervention' (Allen 2011) and 'early help' (Munro 2011b). Allen uses capitals for 'Early Intervention' to stress its importance. He defines this term as follows: 'In this report I wish to reserve the term Early Intervention for the general approaches and the specific policies and programmes which are known to produce the benefits described here for children aged 0–3 and for older children up to 18 who will become better parents of tomorrow' (Allen 2011: xi).

Munro, by contrast, self-consciously uses the term 'early help', stating that she values 'systems theory to examine how the current conditions have evolved' (Munro 2011b: 6). This systems approach recognizes the chains of causality and unintended consequences, providing a method of bringing together a variety of factors: 'Helping children is a human process. When the bureaucratic aspects of work become too dominant, the heart of the work is lost. The recommendations are to be considered together, and the review cautions strongly against cherry picking reforms to implement' (Munro 2011b: 10).

Munro's (2011b) use of the term 'early help', as opposed to the phrase 'early intervention', is anything but semantic. Throughout the report, it is clear that the description of provision of early help, whilst comparable with Allen's (2011) in its recommending joined-up service delivery and using evidence-based approaches, differs in its fundamental aim of how to deliver services. The centrality of her idea of early help is seen in the following recommendation: 'This review is recommending the Government place a duty on local authorities and their statutory partners to secure the sufficient provision of local early help services for children, young people, and their families' (Munro 2011b: 7).

Munro stresses the case for early help as offering both assistance early in a child's life and providing help at the early stages of a problem. The Munro report emphasizes that early help should not be focused on just preventing abuse or neglect but on improving the welfare of children and young people in general. It is also clear that supporting and helping families can only be carried out in partnership, which is why the positive use of the term 'help', rather than 'intervention', is significant. This is consistent with the features of family support as outlined in our introduction to this book. Help suggests service-user consent, whereas intervention clearly does not.

Allen's (2011) recommendations are based on the key role of the foundation years, an emphasis on education, rigorous assessment of child development, nationwide parenting programmes and the implementation of early intervention and evidence-based programmes. The style of the key recommendations, in comparison to Munro, is technocratic, emphasizing stress regulation and heavy state intervention in family life through a tightly focused workforce: 'I recommend that we improve workforce capability of those working with the 0–5s . . . I recommend all key professionals are made aware of the importance of building on the social and emotional capabilities of all children and promoting good parenting through refocused training' (Allen 2011: xix).

Thus the deployment of the terms 'early intervention' and 'early help' are significantly different: in summary, we may say that we associate early intervention with a strong state, technocratic approach, whilst early help is more resonant of consent and partnership with families.

> **Point for reflection:** Reflect on the discussion of 'early help' and 'early intervention': do you prefer one term over the other? If so why?

## Developing service delivery

Since the Children Act 1989 called for increasingly 'joined-up' service delivery and the emergence of a continuum of services to meet the identified needs of children, family support for 'children in need' has had significant legislative backing. This provision recognized that over time complex needs may necessitate a range of services from a variety of agencies. Little supports this, reiterating that 'it does not help, therefore, to place health services in opposition to social services or day care against residential care since all may be a necessary part of a child's recovery' (1999: 307). Currently, the two crucial policy documents we have mentioned that are central to this debate, Allen's (2011) *Early Intervention: The Next Steps* and Munro's (2011b) *The Munro Review of Child Protection: A Child-Centred System*, highlight and compound the different approaches to service delivery. Allen emphasizes programmatic approaches whereas Munro (2011b) illustrates the need for multi-agency, multi-level approaches to a complex child protection system. The Allen review can be seen as approaching prevention in an atomistic way, preventing 'service involvement', whereas Munro is more a holistic perspective, focused on building resilience, as well as addressing children in need through a continuum of service delivery that is multifaceted.

Evidence of this difference can be seen in Allen's recommended nineteen programmes that we discuss further in chapter 3 (Allen 2011). Due to the focus on evidence-based programmes, the Allen review examines a narrow, empirical notion of effectiveness. Thus, for example, there are few programmes in the review's 'top 19 list' for addressing such crucial issues as the impact of substances or stress in pregnancy, breastfeeding and healthy relationships between mother, father and baby, or the many existing comprehensive, evidence-based programmes for those aged five years and over (Centre for Social Justice 2011: 11).

Dunst (1985, 2000) points out that historically early intervention encompassed universal support without an emphasis on professionals and was defined as a 'provision of support to families of infants and young children from members of informal and formal social support networks' (1985: 179). A culture shift has now emerged through the development of Allen's review and others that propose a more targeted, resource- and outcomes-driven approach.

It is likely that fiscal constraint forms the thrust behind the argument for this type of targeting as it supports the position that targeting resources at the most needy is crucial for improving cost-effectiveness of public spending and social intervention. Demographic shifts, the impact of globalization and widespread lack of employment present fiscal challenges to universal provision. Debates about the choice between universalism and targeting centre on the idea of redistribution: that is, that universalism is not truly redistributive. However, many believe that, in most examples, targeting inevitably leads to a reduction in budgets devoted to poverty and welfare and that an increase in the needs of the most vulnerable is actually created by the reduction in the resources allocated to them and the inevitable association with stigma and sometimes means-testing (Hatherley 2011).

> **Point for reflection:** In your experience what impact has there been from the period of 'austerity' on familes and on family support services?

## The use of evidence-based programmes

The importance of acknowledging other types of evidence and not only the 'rigorous' processes promoted in Allen's review (2011) is explored in chapter 3 of this book. There are certainly tensions between Munro and Allen in the use of evidence. Munro's review recommends an orientation towards holistic approaches to early intervention that incorporate the need for shifts in service delivery, multi-agency working and varying professional capacities, while Allen, in his focus on early years, seemingly authorizes a programmatic emphasis by promoting investment in a narrow range of programmes (Centre for Social Justice 2011). These are fundamentally different approaches.

As we explored in chapter 1, early intervention can be understood as an explicit focus on the evidence-based programmes outlined in the Allen report designed to tackle 'problems' defined by professionals in order to prevent the development of issues such as abuse, neglect and poor life outcomes for children and families (Centre for Social Justice 2011). As national definitions of family support, early intervention and early help continue to emerge, it becomes increasingly clear that the subtle differences in the language used highlight major differences in the approaches recommended and supported.

In theory, the government supported and approved the recommendations (Department for Education 2011) by Munro. However, as the political and economic environment changes, the profile of child protection looks as unclear as ever, and early help seems to have been overshadowed by other developments, not least the replacement of the Department for Children, Schools and Families (DCSF) by the Department for Education (DfE) (BBC News 2010). An authoritarian strand can be detected in coalition policy, such as the Children and Families Act 2014's emphasis on 'fast track' adoption and the then minister Michael Gove's speech on the child protection system which categorically stated that more children need to be taken into care (Gove 2012), as well as the nationwide 'Troubled Families' initiative (Casey 2012). None of these approaches seem to coincide with the intentions of the Munro report (2011b) and the 'early help' agenda.

Firstly, the language used by government to define early help is significant: 'Providing early help is more effective in promoting the welfare of children than reacting later. Early help means providing support as soon as a problem emerges, at any point in a child's life, from the foundation years through to the teenage years' (HM Government 2013: 11). The government response also clarifies that early help addresses emerging problems and unmet needs, establishing the language for a holistic approach to child welfare. In particular, it states that 'children and families may need support from a wide range of local agencies' and that provision should 'form part of a continuum of help and support to respond to different levels of need of individual children and families' (HM Government 2013: 14). The government therefore recognizes the importance of multi-professional working and the variety of support needed, as we explore in chapter 10 of this book. This also addresses Theme 2 of the government's response to Munro which sought to share the responsibility of early help (Department for Education 2011: 20) and seems to be a positive step in recognizing the wide scale of support needed. The language used throughout is child-centred, including the widest definition of safeguarding that is used: 'Safeguarding children – the action we take to promote the welfare of children and protect them from harm' (HM Government 2013: 7).

Significantly, the use of this definition moves away from a reactive approach to child protection; rather, it is a description of a shift towards a holistic and proactive perspective on child welfare in a widest sense. There is a strong emphasis on valuing the expertise of professional social workers, particularly as it is specified that a local authority social worker should make the decisions as to the type of response needed from a referral (HM Government 2013: 23). This is also consistent with Theme 1 of the government's response to Munro, which is to value professional expertise.

However, whilst there are some advances from the use of language and emphasis in the early help approach, the overall guidance is not radical enough for the extent of wide-scale reform needed to effectively reduce the level of bureaucracy, as promised in the Munro report. Whilst the previous statutory timescales have been removed, along with the distinction between initial and core assessments, these have been replaced with the '45 working-day timescale', which contradicts the argument for removing prescribed national timescales.

There is an overly weighted emphasis on assessment, including 'early help assessment' (HM Government 2013), as well as numerous prescriptive flowcharts and procedures. All of this seems to contrast with the rhetoric around the empowerment of professionals to enable them to build relationships with children and families, and not to have processes and timescales prescribed by central government.

Additionally, whilst early help is emphasized, so are outcomes (HM Government 2013: 13), thus perhaps echoing the bureaucratic audit and outcome culture of New Labour. Whilst it is important to measure the impact on the child and family, and remain focused on providing effective support, the emphasis is on outcome-measured services, with stringent eligibility through examples such as the 'Troubled Families' initiative, which can contradict the early help agenda. For example, the thresholds document described in *Working Together to Safeguard Children* (HM Government 2013: 14) has initiated further eligibility criteria, in which targeted services are justified at the expense of a wider welfare service delivery.

Furthermore, the changes to the way in which serious case reviews (SCRs) in England are published and monitored are significant in terms of the early help agenda. A national panel of independent experts has been established to advise Local Safeguarding Children Boards (LSCBs) with regard to the initiation and publication of SCRs (HM Government 2013: 69). This has introduced an additional level of decision making, as well as reducing the independence of the LSCBs. The National Panel will also encourage the publication of SCRs in full. The high profile of SCRs tends to contribute to a reactive and defensive professional approach, in which it is difficult for early help to develop and flourish. Reports on child deaths have historically tended to dominate legislation, service delivery and practice, a trend likely to be strengthened by publication in full. This situation varies within the United Kingdom, where England places a higher emphasis on reports about child deaths, meaning that family support is possibly better able to flourish in parts of the United Kingdom other than England.

In summary, *Working Together to Safeguard Children* (HM Government 2013) contains potentially conflicting messages. Although some aspects are promising for the concept of early help, many contradictions and challenges remain. 'Working Together' and the associated Ofsted inspection can be viewed as Munro's swan song: 'what was once a loud and hopeful voice for children and families is in danger of being dominated and diminished by an authoritarian agenda of inspection and regulation' (see Blyth 2014 for a discussion of these issues). The Munro process started strongly and disappeared quickly. 'Working Together' demonstrates that some progressive themes have survived, yet they are nowhere near as holistic and radical as needed for a wide-scale, family support-based reform programme. Although Munro commented that the revisions were a 'very good compromise', it seems as though the rhetoric and the reality of policy are worlds apart.

## Conclusion

We have seen in this chapter that there is a conceptual tussle taking place between the key terms:

- prevention;
- family support;
- early intervention;
- early help.

We have argued, and will continue to do so throughout this book, that, despite its conceptual weakness, 'family support' is the most useful approach to working with children and families. Whilst prevention is too reactive, early intervention is too authoritarian and 'technicist' in its approach. This leaves family support and early help as potentially progressive and helpful concepts. For the authors of this book, 'family support' is more suggestive of working together and partnership than is the concept of 'early help' favoured by Munro.

*Exercise*

Use the material in this chapter to consider how the terms 'family support', 'early intervention' and 'early help' are utilized in child welfare. If you are working alone, consider the strengths and weaknesses of each concept. If you are working in a group, this can be set up as a debate. Give each group the relevant section from the chapter and ask them to argue in favour of one particular definition: family support, early intervention or early help. Take a vote at the end on which concept the participants prefer.

*Discussion*

When the authors undertook the debate above, 'family support' was the most popular term: in practice, 'early help' seems to be the most widely used. We argue throughout this book that how these concepts are used really matters and has an impact on policy and practice.

## Selected further reading

Allen, G. (2011) *Early Intervention: The Next Steps.* London: The Stationery Office. The key influential report – explored in this chapter – which has helped to establish the terms of current family support debates.

Blyth, M. (2014) *Moving on from Munro: Improving Children's Services.* Bristol: Policy Press. An up-to-date edited collection exploring the state of child protection after Munro.

Munro, E. (2011) *The Munro Review of Child Protection: A Child-Centred System.* London: DfE. In some ways, the 'sister' to the Allen report – but with a contrasting approach to some of the key issues, as discussed in this chapter.

# 3 Researching Family Support: Process and Outcomes

Researching family support, or indeed forms of prevention, across a number of social practices presents particular challenges. Essentially, the research task in relation to family support is to ask what has been prevented by a particular policy or practice, thus posing a forward-looking, complex and challenging issue for the research community.

As one would expect, family support research utilizes a range of methods: qualitative, quantitative and mixed-method studies can all be found. Small, qualitative studies, case studies and project evaluations predominate: randomized controlled trials (RCTs) exist but are rare in the United Kingdom, although they are more frequently used in the United States. Some researchers, as we shall see later, have adopted a 'futures methodology' to address the researching future-prevention challenge mentioned above. It will be argued here that seemingly abstract debates over research methods truly matter in the field of family support: these debates have a direct impact on policy, funding and practice, as we shall witness throughout this book.

The aim of this chapter is to explore the challenge of researching family support and to understand why the debates already briefly outlined actually matter. First of all, we will explore the range of methods adopted in family support studies. We will move on to case studies of family support research in order to provide a discussion of the 'state of the art'. Finally, we will speculate on the future of family support research and how it can take forward the historical, policy and theoretical discussions rehearsed in Part I of this book.

> **Point for reflection:** How does research influence your practice? How do you access up-to-date research? Do you need to improve your access to research?

## Family support: methods and approaches

Family support is essentially a human and relational process (see chapter 8 of this book): it is concerned with the actions and practices of families being supported and those of the professionals and occasional volunteers who work with them. In this book, we maintain that the emphasis on 'outcomes' (the measurable results of family support) has rather undermined a focus on the 'process' (the means by which human beings undertake the tasks) involved in family support. It is argued here that we need to put due emphasis on both factors – 'outcomes' and 'process' – if we are to fully understand the complexities and nuances of family support: 'In any evaluation of family support, a balance must be struck between the demands of technically achievable, objective measures and the need to adequately represent and address the fundamental purpose of policy and practice' (Pinkerton and Katz 2003: 16).

By rehabilitating the focus on process in this way, we also in turn rescue qualitative studies, which provide insight into how people experience service delivery. Qualitative studies enable us to reflect on the narrative of service users – for them to explain in their own words how they experience family support services. Such studies can adopt a range of techniques: unstructured, semi-structured, structured interviews, some forms of surveys and also observational methods are helpful. These approaches do not necessarily have to concern themselves with the rigorous measurement of outcomes or cost-benefits in the way that quantitative studies do. Unfortunately, the current fetish for 'systematic review' often, rather arrogantly, dismisses these studies.

Qualitative studies often provide a direct voice for the service user. They are consistent with family support values, which is important, as Weiss states: 'The service delivery values and principles behind family support are challenging evaluators in many countries to experiment with different evaluation approaches and measures' (Weiss 2003: xvi). Consistent with family support values, qualitative methods allow researchers to present the feelings, experiences and perspectives of the service user and to accept these as valid in their own right, without the support of statistical methods or a narrative of objectivity and statistical validity. Given that family support is essentially a human process, this is an important goal of research. Of course, this is not an excuse for weak research methodology or design. Dolan, Canavan, and Pinkerton make the case for reflective practice, informed by research, in relation to family support: 'Doing family support requires a mixture of description and questioning informed by action. It is a mixture which provides the basis for reflective practice' (2006: 17).

As Godar points out, family support research can play a range of useful roles in planning service development including the exploration of:

- Prevalence: how many children and families have a particular characteristic, or experience (e.g. number of children living with domestic violence).
- Trends: is the number of children with a particular need changing over time? Are the types of needs that children experience changing?
- Relationships: is there a relationship between different characteristics and needs (e.g. the correlation between parental substance misuse and domestic violence)? Where a robust statistical analysis is carried out and shows a relationship between two factors, this is called correlation.

- Risk: does the presence of a particular need, or combination of needs, increase the probability of a later negative outcome (e.g. the increased risk that the children of young parents will not reach developmental milestones by the age of five)? (2013: 42)

## Evidence, RCTs and family support

In recent decades, two approaches have become increasingly dominant in debates about the impact of family support: one discourse has focused on RCTs as the 'gold standard' of research and the other on early brain development. These two discourses will be reflected upon and challenged in this section.

These two discourses – RCTs and brain development – came together in a highly influential report commissioned by the then newly elected British coalition government which we discussed in chapters 1 and 2. The report – *Early Development: The Next Steps* (2011) – was prepared by (an Opposition) Labour MP, Graham Allen. Allen had worked for some time at the Centre for Social Justice with Iain Duncan Smith, who was later to become the 2010–2015 coalition government's Work and Pensions Minister. The Allen report makes a strong case for 'early intervention' as defined and discussed in the first two chapters of this book. The front cover of the report was graphically illustrated with a reproduction of a 'healthy' child's brain and a 'neglected' child's brain. This illustration has become iconic and is often cited and reproduced at professional conferences and networks.

The use of these brain illustrations has been challenged. In a journalistic context, the *Guardian* commentator Zoe Williams says: 'I believe it [the illustration] to have had as much egregious influence on the way the early years debate has been framed as the 45-minute claim for Saddam Hussein's weapons capability had on the Iraq war debate' (Williams 2013).

Academic commentators Wastell and White argue along similar lines, claiming that the promoters of the significance of brain development 'appear to be operating as powerful "trump cards" in what is actually very contentious terrain, suppressing vital *moral* debate regarding the shape of state interventions in the lives of children and families' (Wastell and White 2012: 399). Similarly, too, Munro and Musholt claim that '[t]he findings from neuroscience research on the neurological impact of maltreatment are being seized on with enthusiasm as showing hard and compelling evidence of the damage children suffer' (2013: 1).

Wastell and White and Williams further argue that the shrivelled brain illustration depicts severe 'global neglect', rather than the more usual 'chaotic neglect' that family support practitioners are more likely to come across in modern welfare states. In fact, in contrast to the strong case put by the Allen report, 'neuroscientific knowledge is at an early and provisional stage' (Wastell and White 2012: 407). This is a serious challenge to the utilization of an illustration that is often referred to in British family support discourse. The case is overstated according to Sir Michael Rutter, a leading

British authority in child development: 'As several commentators have pointed out, the claims are misleading and fallacious . . . and the assumption that later experiences necessarily have only minor effects is clearly wrong' (Rutter in Wastell and White 2012: 404).

A later, more extensive article by Williams (2014) in the *Guardian* newspaper led to an extended series of letters to the newspaper, including correspondence supporting a sceptical stance to brain research from an eminent brain researcher, Professor Steven Rose (*Guardian*, 30 April 2014), who considers that the use of the brain illustration by Allen is a 'travesty of what neuroscience can and cannot say about early child development. The image derives from a short unrefereed report from a US neuroscience meeting, without information as to its provenance.'

Williams quotes an eminent brain researcher as follows:

> Bruer says his interest is apolitical, and is in how much we can actually tell from the evidence we're given. 'The first three years of life is a period of rapid synaptic development. But what this implies for brain function and behaviour is only asserted by early-years advocates: cue the erroneous conclusion that human brain development is effectively solidified by the end of the first three years.' It is true, he points out later, that the brain is 80% of its full size by the end of your third year; 'what this tells us about brain function is precisely nothing.' (Williams 2014)

Munro and Musholt reach a nuanced summary following their critical review of brain research. They conclude that 'Neuroscientific studies need to be based on, and developed in concert with, social scientific theories if they are to truly advance our understanding. We suggest that this can best be achieved by integrating findings from neuroscience into the existing broader ecological framework for the study of maltreatment' (Munro and Musholt 2013: 9).

Thus we have good reason to be sceptical about brain research influencing child welfare policy and practice.

> **Point for reflection:** Have you been taught about or otherwise heard about brain research and how it is important for family work? What is your opinion?

Regardless of any critique of brain science, there can be little doubt that the Allen report was highly influential and, as we shall see, had a direct impact on commissioning and policy through its championing of nineteen programmes that it held up as being clearly evidenced and therefore more reliable and offering value for money for early intervention commissioners. The nineteen programmes are reproduced in the box overleaf.

The commitment to these programmes is based on a wide range of aspirations and ideologies outlined by Allen as follows:

> Early Intervention is an approach which offers our country a real opportunity to make lasting improvements in the lives of our children, to forestall many persistent social problems and end their transmission

**The Nineteen Programmes Recommended by the Allen Report**

Curiosity Corner (as part of Success for All)
Early Literacy and Learning Model (ELLM)
Functional Family Therapy (FFT)
Incredible Years
Let's Begin with the Letter People
Life Skills Training (LST)
Lions Quest Skills for Adolescence
Multidimensional Treatment Foster Care (MTFC)
Multi-systemic Therapy (MST)
Nurse Family Partnership (NFP)
Parent–Child Home Program
Project Towards No Drug Abuse (Project TND)
Promoting Alternative Thinking Strategies (PATHS)
Reading Recovery
Ready, Set, Leap!
Safe Dates
Safer Choices
Start Taking Alcohol Risks Seriously (STARS) for Families
Success for All

from one generation to the next, and to make long-term savings in public spending. It covers a range of tried and tested policies for the first three years of children's lives to give them the essential social and emotional security they need for the rest of their lives. It also includes a range of well-established policies for when they are older which leave children ready to face the challenges of each stage of childhood and of passage into adulthood – especially the challenge of becoming good parents to their own children. (Allen 2011: vii)

We can see that Allen bases his arguments firmly in evidence without, perhaps, recognizing how contested and complex this evidence is. The quote also illustrates that family support debates have a resonance well beyond the child welfare community: Allen clearly links these policy debates to issues such as patterns of public expenditure. The policy focus on childhood and early intervention has become heightened, it can be argued, by the impact of globalization and the focus on childhood as a period of investment essential to a nation's success in a period of intense global economic competitiveness (Frost 2011). Early intervention is perceived by Allen not just as an approach, but as the answer: 'a range of well-tested programmes, low in cost, high in results, can have a lasting impact on all children, especially the most vulnerable' (Allen 2011: ix).

As we stated earlier, this is a 'technicist' approach in the true sense of the word – where complex human processes are seen as being grasped and indeed transformed by evidenced technical programmes and interventions. The evaluation of such early years interventions should be read with caution as the 'results provide neither evidence that irreversible brain damage has been prevented, nor evidence that the first three years are critical in terms of neural development, nor do they purport to do so' (Wastell and White 2012: 405).

In contrast to this sceptical approach, the Allen report draws on the neurological evidence that we have discussed earlier as if it were conclusive:

> We have attempted to present the overwhelming scientific evidence that the first years of a child's life are essential to the development of their brain and, especially, their social and emotional capabilities. This development depends vitally on a baby's formation of a close and trusting bond with at least one main carer. Failure to develop such a bond can have dire lifelong consequences, both for individuals and societies. Unless and until we recognise the way major problems are formed early in people's lives, no amount of well-intentioned policy or initiatives will succeed in reducing them. (Allen 2011: 17)

This faith in evidence is, however, based in a blinkered 'technical-rationalist' approach, and on a belief in some of the programmes, which raises an issue of the transferability of evidence across the Atlantic from the United States, where most of it originates. Allen is aware that 'Too few of the Early Intervention programmes currently being tried in the UK have been rigorously evaluated, making it difficult for the public sector and impossible for the private sector to invest with any confidence' (Allen 2011: 68).

This rather adds to Allen's problems – where a reliance on contested evidence is compounded by a faith in the geographical and social transferability of this evidence. Allen is aware of this challenge and reflects on this situation as follows:

> Readers will have noticed that many of the programmes selected by the review team have their origins outside the UK, mostly in the US. This does not reflect any lack of innovation in the field of Early Intervention in this country. On the contrary, during the review and in the preparation of my book with Iain Duncan Smith, I have been constantly impressed with the potential for voluntary and statutory organizations to develop ingenious ideas to help our children. But we have lagged behind other countries in the rigorous development and testing of those ideas. (Allen 2011: 76)

We maintain that family support is about more than a 'programmatic' fix to social problems. This indeed has been one of the problems with the unquestioning import of United States-based evidence. The welfare state infrastructure in the United States is minimal, compared to that in the United Kingdom. Even after a period of 'austerity' and retrenchment, the UK welfare state still has elements of universalism that will not be found in the United States. This fundamentally changes the nature of family support programmes. Whereas in the United Kingdom these programmes supplement universal approaches (to health, income support and day care), in the United States families are more dependent on family support programmes as the mainstay of their functioning. This social context should make us wary of the unquestioning transfer of programmes and evidence from the United States context.

Thus there is a problem with the importation of research findings. Allen argues for his selected nineteen programmes, using four criteria:

- Evaluation quality – favouring those early interventions that have been evaluated to a very high standard, using the most robust evaluation methods, such as randomized controlled trials or quasi-experimental techniques, and ideally summarized in systematic reviews.
- Impact – favouring those early interventions that have a positive impact on children's health and development and particularly their social and emotional competences.
- Intervention specificity – favouring those early interventions that are clear about what they are intending to achieve, for whom, why, how and where. Much of the evaluation literature has shown clarity on this dimension to be a key characteristic of successful interventions. It is also an essential ingredient to the economic appraisal of programmes.
- System readiness – favouring those early interventions that can be effectively integrated in the wider public service infrastructure and are supported by a strategy for ensuring that potential economic benefits can be realized. (Allen 2011: 69)

Since coming up with this very bold and powerfully stated 'scientific' approach to early intervention, it is clear that the Centre for Social Justice (CSJ) – the original champions of 'early intervention' – became afraid of the impact of the Allen report and the privileging of the nineteen evidence-based programmes. The CSJ report, *Making Sense of Early Intervention*, represents a major step back from the rhetoric around brain development and RCTs, and acts as an effective challenge to the Allen report. The impact of the report and the enthusiasm of the CSJ in stepping back from this is more than apparent in the following explanation, which is worth quoting at length:

> It is clear that there is an impressive level of consensus about where our focus needs to be and what needs to be changed in our delivery. However, a similar consensus is less apparent in where investment would best be made: on which programmes and approaches are most deserving of funding. Many local authorities have recently begun to focus their expenditure more or less exclusively on the Allen Review's 19 top-tier programmes, treating the endorsement they are given in the report as a 'top down' directive when, with this Government's emphasis on local decision making, this was not the intention. We have heard of existing interventions, both early years and school age, previously endorsed by commissioners because of their proven track record now being discontinued because they are not on the list of 19 'approved' programmes. Many have been cited by reviewers as having unimpeachable evidence of effectiveness. (Centre for Social Justice 2011: 8)

Clearly, the CSJ is gravely concerned about the impact of the Allen report and seems keen to distance itself from the negative and undesirable impact it has had in places.

We are left with a major challenge for family support policy and practice. There has been an unseemly embrace of brain research and United States-based evidence which has led to commissioners adopting programmes with over-inflated claims of rigour. In this book, we are in favour of a more socially situated, process-sensitive approach which recognizes the importance of the day-to-day qualitative experiences of service users. It is important that these lived experiences are not reduced to 'outcomes' in a mechanical and 'technicist' manner.

## Randomized controlled trials

In medicine and health studies, the 'gold standard' for research is the randomized controlled trial (RCT). Many readers will be aware that, when a new drug has been developed, it will often be tested on two groups: individuals will be randomly assigned to these groups. One group will be administered the new drug, the others will then normally be given a placebo (a sugar tablet, for example) that contains nothing that is medically beneficial. The outcomes for each group will then be measured. Statistical methods are used to assess whether the drug has had a significant impact, and therefore whether it is worthy of further development and prescription.

This method has champions in the field of social science. They contend that, if social science is a 'science' worthy of the term, it should adopt similar scientific method. For example, a parenting programme could be administered to one group, and not to another randomly assigned control group. According to the RCT followers, we can then measure the impact of the intervention: 'The RCT is the best method to assess a causal relationship between intervention and outcome' (Torgerson and Torgerson 2008: 2). Torgerson and Torgerson also claim that:

> random assignment acts like a lottery and results in equal distribution between the groups – programme and control – of the variables that might affect outcomes. Any chance differences between the groups in observable variance can be corrected using regression analytical techniques. Other methods ... [s]uch as pre- and post-test or statistical matching may result in biased answers due to problems of temporal change or confounding. (2008: 2)

This assumed methodological superiority is summarized by these authors as follows: 'The superiority of the RCT over most methods of impact evaluation lies in the fact that unknown or unmeasured variables will be equally distributed between groups' (Torgerson and Torgerson 2008: 2).

Many proponents of RCT are 'hard-line' in their support for rigour in research design, as illustrated by the following:

> Comparison groups constructed using samples of convenience – such as groups consisting of participants who stop taking part, participants who

take part infrequently, children whose parents express interest but elect not to participate, or children who are eligible and whose parents do not express interest – are likely to fall short of desired standards of rigour. Decisions by these groups indicate that they differ from participants who continued within the programme. (Dynarski and Del Grosso 2008: 11)

It should be noted that supporters of qualitative methods tend to be less dogmatic and tend to recognize the role of more quantitative methods if appropriately applied.

One objection to RCTs in the human sciences is that they exclude the control group from service provision. The supporters of RCTs respond to moral critiques about excluding potential participants as follows:

Random assignment is fair because it gives all participants a chance of being selected for the programme. Personal or judgment factors play no role in whether a participant is selected. Programmes often have more applicants than they are able to serve and using random assignment is the same as picking names from a hat or using a lottery to allocate limited programme spaces. (Dynarski and Del Grosso 2008: 11)

In addition, supporters of RCTs also often make a strong case for increasing expenditure on social research:

RCTs of social interventions are complex. They can be harder to deliver, and considerably more expensive than other forms of outcome study such as one-group post-test only designs. Yet in the UK, funding for social care research has amounted to little more than 'small chance' compared with budgets for healthcare research. For example, the pricing of even a small health enquiry (such as – taking one example with which I am familiar – the collection and analysis of blood samples at two or three time points from around 80 children) is likely to be set at levels well above acceptable social work research grants. (Macdonald 2008: 32)

However, we can argue that the social world is not amenable to the same form of measurement as the medical world. In medicine one can suppose that the benefits are clear and have some universal assent. For example, if the impact of arthritis has been reduced, we can all welcome this because a reduction in pain is desirable. The social world is, however, more complex. First, the changes may be more problematic and debatable: what does good parenting look like, for example? Some may favour more permissive parenting; others may prefer more authoritative parenting (see chapter 6 of this book). Even if we can agree what 'good parenting' looks like, it is harder to measure such a complex social practice. In addition, there are moral challenges. By creating a control group, we are also denying a group access to a service which may in the extreme lead to the death or impairment of a child. One major third-sector organization with which one of the authors worked declined an RCT of their work on this moral basis. Thus some would claim that the RCT is not immediately transferable to the social world. We can also ask if RCTs can measure complex issues of process and support offered by family support projects. For example, one of the authors interviewed a Somalian refugee mother about her experience of a children's centre. She said that she valued the centre as 'I used to cry alone and now I have many shoulders to cry on'. Statements such as this are not amenable to outcome measures or RCTs but express the value of family support services. This statement also provides an emphasis on process (how we do things) rather than any measurable change or outcome.

The respected analyst of family support research, James Heckman, makes the following observations and summarizes a sceptical attitude to RCTs:

> An uncritical reliance on evidence from randomised control trials is not good science. Experiments can answer a limited number of relevant questions. They do not illuminate the mechanisms producing the effects that are presented. They do not inform their relevance to other environments or to related programs. Most pernicious they promote the fallacy of searching under the streetlight: what is not studied by a randomised trial is not considered worthy of attention even if a large body of hard science and common sense suggests otherwise. Used in this way, the appeal to experiments as the gold standard or the only standard is an excuse for not thinking hard or doing hard science. (Heckman 2005: 2)

We should, therefore, be sceptical of the value of RCTs in family support: whilst they may have a role, we also require more nuanced and wide-ranging social scientific methods. As Featherstone and her colleagues point out:

> In the international family support literature, there is a refreshing degree of attention paid to thinking about what kinds of support activities are valued and make a difference to families with emphasis on the local and the innovating as well as the large scale (Dolan, Canavan and Pinkerton 2006). Reflective practice has been written into policy agendas in countries such as the Republic of Ireland in order to ensure a project that's rooted in on-going learning. Such learning is valued above fidelity to programme (Dolan et al. 2006). Whilst some of this has been drawn on in the UK to inform family support activities, there has been such a preference for 'evidence based' transportable programmes that innovation and diversity have been frowned upon. (Featherstone, White and Morris 2014: 11)

**Point for reflection:** Consider the strengths and weaknesses of the RCT-based approach to family support research using the material in this chapter. What is your opinion on the value of RCTs?

## A 'futures' methodology

We have seen that there are number of challenges in researching family support. We can ask a number of complex questions that have no easy answers:

- How can we research what has been prevented?
- Can randomized controlled trials be utilized?

- Can evidence be transferred across international boundaries and contexts?

We will now discuss the 'futures methodology' used to address the challenge of researching family support.

Amongst the most important recent studies regarding family support are those undertaken by a local authority-funded organization known as LARC (the Local Authority Research Consortium). There are five studies to date produced on family support, as shown in the box below:

---

### The LARC studies of family support

Lord, P., Kinder, K., Wilkin, A., Atkinson, M. and Harland, J. (2008) *Evaluating the Early Impact of Integrated Children's Services: Round 1 Final Report.* Slough: NFER.

Easton, C., Morris, M. and Gee, G. (2010) *LARC 2: Integrated Children's Services and the CAF Process.* Slough: NFER.

Easton, C., Gee, G., Durbin, B. and Teeman, D (2011) *Early Intervention, using the CAF Process, and its Cost Effectiveness: Findings from LARC 3.* Slough: NFER.

Easton, C., Featherstone G., Poet, H., Aston, H., Gee, G. and Durbin, B. (2012) *Supporting Families with Complex Needs: Findings from LARC 4. Slough: NFER.*

Easton, C., Lamont, L., Smith, R. and Aston, H. (2013) *'We Should Have Been Helped from Day One': A Unique Perspective from Children, Families and Practitioners: Findings from LARC 5.* Slough: NFER.

For the sake of brevity in the following discussion, we shall refer to these important studies in turn as LARC 1, LARC 2, LARC 3, LARC 4 and LARC 5.

---

The LARC 1 study aimed to identify the early impact of integrated children's services and the features that promote or hinder success in improving outcomes for children and young people. The research operated in a variety of localities within fourteen participating areas, with one locality being chosen as the focus within each area. Children, young people and parents in this study report a range of improvements in outcomes as a result of the support they received. The most common improvements in outcomes noted by children and young people are the following: getting on well with schoolwork; feeling safer; and feeling happier. Parents also report their child's enhanced confidence or self-esteem. The LARC 1 study authors deem that it is important for children's services leadership teams to give early attention to the development of robust and comparable measures of children's emotional health and well-being.

The LARC 2 study reported findings supplied by twenty-four local authorities using the Common Assessment Framework (CAF), a method of offering early help to families in need. The study suggests that the CAF appears to be supporting improved outcomes for children, young people and families but notes that more needs to be done to embed the CAF as a tool for supporting early intervention and prevention.

Three areas that require action are suggested by the LARC 2 study:

1. Clear commitment and action from Children's Trust Boards to support the effective operation of the CAF process across all partner agencies.
2. A clear policy for how the 'lead professional' role is allocated and supported, including the possibility of a new identified workforce of professionals dedicated to this role (see chapter 11 of this book).
3. Absolute clarity on what the Assessment Framework is, who it is for and how this relates to other formal assessments undertaken by partner agencies.

These requirements for action suggest that there is a need for dedicated assessment practitioners to develop further professional expertise for family support. Further, it is argued that guidance and thresholds of needs can be problematic to apply (see chapter 1), and that assessment practitioners may not fully understand that any other formal assessment undertaken for a child can be incorporated within the CAF assessment by creating a single, working document that can reduce bureaucracy and provide a comprehensive, holistic picture of the child and their world.

The next study, known as LARC 3, documents local research projects covering twenty-one local authority areas. The LARC 3 study finds that 'the costs invested in assessments and interventions identified in the LARC cases are consistently and significantly lower than the future costs avoided'. This finding is consistent with the High Scope/Perry study reported on later in this chapter.

LARC 4 presents findings from twelve local authorities, using thirty-nine case studies. The authors of LARC 4 outline their methodology as follows:

> Eleven of the twelve LARC 4 local authorities carried out their own qualitative case study research projects within an overall agreed framework developed by the LAs [local authorities] and NFER [National Foundation for Educational Research]. Each case study involved interviews with LA practitioners, parents and (where appropriate) children and young people. In all, the LAs conducted around 80 interviews across 39 case studies between spring and autumn 2011. Each case study looked at whether the common assessment process is a cost effective way to support improved outcomes and avoid costly, negative outcomes for families later on. (LARC 4: Summary)

They also explored how to assess the costs and/or savings of implementing the Assessment Framework:

> To calculate a difference in costs (i.e. an indicative 'saving'), LARC adopted the adapted 'futures methodology' used during LARC 3. Futures methodologies are increasingly being used within research and evaluation to ascertain what might happen if, for example, an intervention had not been implemented. LARC 4 LA (local authorities) asked practitioners,

parents and, where appropriate, children/young people for their perceptions on what the life course of a child/family might have been had the
CAF process not been initiated. LARC LA leads then moderated all the
case studies. (LARC 4: Summary)

The main areas of work undertaken in the cases explored were as follows:

- enhance parenting strategies (31 families);
- develop emotional health and resilience (22 families);
- improve engagement in education (18 families);
- engage in positive activities (13 families);
- promote physical health management (11 families). (LARC 4: 7)

The key findings of the LARC 4 study are summarized in the report's
foreword as follows:

- Outcomes for children, young people and their families experiencing
  problems can be improved – and in some cases very dramatically – by
  appropriate interventions planned and managed by services working
  together.
- The Common Assessment Framework process encourages, and provides a good basis for, such integrated planning and intervention.
- There are five key success factors for early intervention, all of which
  should be present.
- The costs of working and intervening in this joined-up way are likely to
  be repaid many times over by the avoidance of greater costs later in life
  of the child or family (although not all of the savings accrue at the local
  service level). (LARC 4: Foreword)

The 'five key success factors' referred to above are:

1. engaging children, young people and families as equal partners in the
   process;
2. ensuring consistency of the lead professional support, which helped
   families and professionals work better together;
3. integrating all the elements of the Common Assessment Framework
   process;
4. ensuring multi-agency working and information sharing, which
   improved understanding of need and service provision;
5. developing a better understanding of children and young people's
   needs at the earliest possible stage. (LARC 4: 21)

The final study explored here, LARC 5, aims to offer 'a unique insight'
into the views of children, young people and their parents who have been
supported by early intervention services, and others who have received
interventions around child neglect.

In LARC 5, nine local authorities were researched around the question:
'How do we effectively support families with different levels of need across
the early intervention spectrum to engage with services within an overall
framework of neglect?' Utilizing a similar approach as the Hardiker Model

discussed earlier in this book (see chapter 1), the research focused on children experiencing the following levels of neglect:

- Level Two, related to families where the parent/s *mostly* met the child's needs;
- Level Three, where children had some unmet needs; lived in a family home that lacked routines; had parents with poor awareness of safety issues; and the child received limited interaction and affection;
- Level Four, where adults' needs were put before the child's, and where the child had low nutrition and scarce stimulation.

The study does not include more 'heavy-end', 'significant harm' cases. The LARC 5 study collected data was from more than a hundred practitioners from a variety of settings and from forty parents, children and young people. The researchers point out that not all authorities had a clear definition or policy in place to support practitioners to define and identify child neglect (except where chronic neglect was evident). Practitioners said they used their own professional judgement to identify child neglect and seemed to have a good understanding of the risk factors to be aware of. They noted, however, that defining neglect can often be a 'grey area'. Further, they explained that defining neglect needs an element of 'flexibility' within an early intervention context. It needs to take account of individual family circumstances and lifestyles. Where a child was suspected of suffering from chronic neglect, practitioners explained that child protection and safeguarding procedures would be implemented immediately.

Practitioners defined indicators of neglect under four headings: physical neglect; emotional neglect; educational needs; and parental behaviours. Practitioners recognized that it was not always easy to distinguish between physical and emotional neglect as many issues were interrelated. A summary of practitioner views is presented in the box below.

We can see that the LARC studies have made a major contribution to debates about both methodology and outcomes in family support.

---

## LARC Conclusions and Recommendations

The LARC 5 research shows that practitioners and families share common views about how families can be supported. While the research focused on early intervention and child neglect, the noted successes in supporting families, the challenges associated with them and suggestions for making improvements are applicable to supporting any family that needs additional help (not only those experiencing neglect).

The data show that some practitioners would respond to families across all three levels of neglect, while others would not. They felt that most help was available when families encountered more complex difficulties, rather than offering them preventative support through education or universal services. Interestingly, when talking about children experiencing neglect, practitioners talked about the underlying issues, whereas families talked about the symptoms of these issues. This may suggest that more could be done to educate families about neglectful behaviours.

While practice varied between practitioner groups and authorities, some sectors continue not to engage with early intervention and prevention, according to practitioner interview data. In particular, interviewees mentioned the education sector, general practitioners (GPs) not engaging with the CAF process, and a lack of information sharing.

One of the key factors in ensuring families are supported in a timely and effective way, and so do not enter a cycle of needing support (the 'revolving door'), is to offer early intervention and preventative advice and support. Both practitioners and families agreed that more needed to be done to offer help early.

To overcome current gaps and challenges, practitioners and families offered a number of suggestions. Some would require substantial investment (or system change); others were more practical and should be relatively easy to implement. These related to:

- promoting and advertising early help services more effectively to families and practitioners;
- simplifying processes (such as referral route times and the CAF process) and reducing waiting lists;
- improving multi-agency working and information sharing;
- improving families' knowledge about provision of services for children in need and the specialist work of children's social care to help remove the stigma associated with getting help and to allay commonly held misconceptions about child protection and the removal of children from their families;
- considering opportunities for offering families peer to peer support within the community (possibly by training parent volunteers to support families in need);
- undertaking whole family holistic assessments and putting support in place for the whole family, recognizing the value of non-statutory services in helping statutory services to achieve sustained outcomes for children and young people – supporting families to step down from targeted services and avoid a cycle of dependency (the 'revolving door');
- ensuring frontline staff have core skills to help develop and enhance relationships with families.

Authority representatives noted that being involved in LARC 5 had had a positive impact. Some had already made changes to service delivery by applying the lessons learned from the research, while others were making plans to ensure that the learning is taken on board.

**Point for reflection:** How convincing do you find the LARC research? Can it be used to encourage more investment in family support?

## High/Scope Perry Pre-School Program:
## A fortieth birthday follow-up RCT

One creative example of an RCT, with a remarkable follow-up period of interviewing former child participants on their fortieth birthdays, is a United States programme – the High/Scope Perry Pre-School Program. The High/Scope Perry project ran in an inner-city area of Michigan during the 1960s. The programme involved day care and home visiting with a group of African American children, aged between three and five years. There was also a non-intervention group which acted as a control, so that the outcomes of both groups could be compared. The family support programme consisted of two and a half hours day care for the children during the week: this drew on an active learning and child-centred model of family support. This daycare provision was undertaken together with a series of home visits, thus providing a multifaceted intervention programme.

There was an extensive research programme which followed up the children at 15, 19 and 27 years of age and, most recently around their fortieth birthdays. There were 58 children in the original intervention group and 63 in the control group. The drop-out rate was remarkably low: the researchers were in contact with about 90 per cent of the group at the fortieth birthday follow-up.

Drawing from this High/Scope Perry Pre-School Program data and other programmes, Cunha and Heckman claim that 'The most effective supplements supply family resources to young children from disadvantaged environments' (2006: 1). Heckman and his colleagues undertook a secondary analysis of the Perry statistics. Amongst their conclusions is that 'crime reduction is a major benefit of this program' (Heckman et al. 2009: 11).

In a similar vein, Bellfield et al. undertook an overall cost-benefit analysis and estimate that US$12.90 is saved from public costs for every US$1 invested. They claim that 'program gains come mainly from reduced crime by males'. Most commentators, including Cunha and Heckman, argue that the social gains are related to education so that, in American terms, 'completing high school is a major crime prevention strategy' (Bellfield, Noves and Barrett 2006: 60).

We can see, then, that outcomes can be measured where there is a control group and where sufficient research resources are allocated to allow a follow-up study – a remarkable period in this study with a fortieth birthday follow-up.

The Scottish government utilizes these arguments in support of its own early years' interventions in Scotland where, it maintains, a 'wide-range of economic studies suggest that returns to early investment in children during the pre-birth period and up to the age of eight years are high . . . there are greater returns to be sought from identifying and targeting interventions in early childhood for disadvantaged children' (Scottish Government 2010).

## Conclusion

In this chapter, we have explored the issues and challenges of researching family support. We have argued that research has a real and important impact on the field of family support: research really matters. We have also claimed that the family support research is in danger of being dominated by two discourses: one theme being around brain research and the other around the use of RCTs as a methodological approach. We have questioned the validity and applicability of these two approaches. We have argued for a more flexible and nuanced approach to family support research and that this should not be disconnected from the social context of family support. There is a clear role for qualitative studies and innovative methods such as 'futures' methodology. We have also warned against 'technicist' approaches which reduce complex human processes to a technical 'fix'. Moral and value-based judgements quite properly are required around family support: it is essentially a human process and therefore requires moral as well as 'scientific' debate.

*Exercise*

Choose a research study relevant to family support – perhaps one mentioned in this chapter. How does the study contribute to developing family support practice? What are the strengths of the study? Are there any weaknesses in the study?

*Discussion*

In this chapter, we have tried to explore the relationship between research and family support policy and practice. Research has a positive role to play, but within the research community there are differences of opinion, for example between those who favour randomized controlled trials (RCTs) and those who are more sceptical. It is important, therefore, that you develop your own perspective on which research you find more useful in your role.

## Selected further reading

Dolan, P., Canavan, J. and Pinkerton, J. (2006) *Family Support and Reflective Practice*. London: Jessica Kingsley Press. A fascinating and influential collection of material which pursues many of the themes explored in this book.

Easton, C., Lamont, L., Smith, R. and Aston, H. (2013) *'We Should Have Been Helped from Day One': A Unique Perspective from Children, Families and Practitioners: Findings from LARC 5*. Slough: NFER. The fifth of a series of reports which make a major contribution to debates about family support and research methods.

# PART II

## DELIVERING FAMILY SUPPORT

In Part II of this book, we explore a number of practices which contribute to the extensive range of practices that make up family support. The six practice areas we explore are: community-based approaches, home visiting, parenting education, targeted programmes, relationship-based practice and family group conferences. We do not mean to imply that these six approaches make up the whole repertoire of family support (that would require many volumes) but they do represent the Hardiker Model as follows:

**Table II.1** Hardiker Model and family support practice

| Level of practice | Practice area* |
| --- | --- |
| Primary | Community-based responses |
| Secondary | Home visiting |
| | Parenting education |
| | Relationship-based approaches |
| Tertiary | Home visiting |
| | Relationship-based approaches |
| | Family group conferences |
| | Targeted approaches |

*Note*: Some practices cross more than one level.

The six chosen practice examples also share our features of family support.

1.  Family support offers inclusive and engaging practices based on the idea of offering support to families and children who feel they require such support. Family support is therefore strongly suggestive of partnership, engagement and consent.

2.  Such support can be offered early in the life of the child or early in the emergence of the identified challenge facing the family. It is important that family support services are relevant to all children and young people, and not only to younger children.

3.  Family support is a proactive process which engages with the parent(s) and/or young person in the process of change. Implicit in the term 'family support' is the suggestion of bringing about change within the family network.

4.  Family support attempts to prevent the emergence, or worsening, of family challenges.

5.  Family support is necessarily based on a theory of change. Any family support intervention should aim to result in some desirable change and draw on a belief that change is achievable.

6.  Family support draws on a diverse 'tool kit' of skills and approaches. It attempts to develop and encourage local, informal support networks.

7.  Family support aims to generate wider social change and benefits. Such results may lead to a saving in public expenditure, a decrease in social problems, an improvement in the quality of family life or a reduction in measurable outcomes, such as the number of children coming into care.

8.  Family support works with children and young people in partnership and encourages and develops their resilience.

Each practice chapter presents the principal features of each practice, provides a case study that applies the practice, includes points for reflection and suggests further reading.

# 4 Community-Based Projects: The Universal Provision of Family Support

In this chapter, we will examine community-based projects as a specific form of family support and analyse in particular the use of children's centres as a community resource for the provision of a *whole family approach* to service delivery. These are the services delivered at the universal, primary prevention level of the Hardiker Model we discussed in chapter 1. We provide a brief overview of the policy context to show how Sure Start children's centres were developed, and discuss the research findings arising from this initiative in order to understand the subsequent developments in children's centres. We will examine the research and theoretical approaches to understanding family support delivery within children's centres, as well as acknowledging the importance of other more specific community projects. We will discuss a case study example, in which family support as a community-based project is being delivered effectively and discuss the most recent policy changes that will impact the future of children's centres. The chapter will illustrate the central importance of the universal provision of family support.

> **Point for reflection:** As a parent or relative, think of a community service used by a child you know. What was the experience of using this service? How could it have been improved?

## Community-based support

There is a near consensus within the child welfare literature that the provision of services in a timely manner, delivered within the local community with minimal stigma, is the most effective way to provide support in order to meet the needs of children and their families (Frost, Lloyd, and Jeffery 2003). As discussed in our first two chapters, family support is a broad, interchangeable and fluid term, but it is often used when describing the characteristics of community-based service provision to families. It is commonly accepted as a partnership way of working with families, as opposed to something done to families, and often encompasses a flexible delivery of provision adaptable to the needs of the local demographic requirements.

Community-based projects are designed to utilize and promote local resources and available support to strengthen families' cohesion and resilience on a universal and non-stigmatizing basis. Putti and Brady discuss community-based family support in the Republic of Ireland as having the aim of '[p]utting in place a family strengths-building programme, through the provision of supports to individual families on the one hand and capacity-building in the community on the other' (Putti and Brady 2011: 273).

Trivette and Dunst (2005) carried out a study of the effectiveness of community-based family support in the United States. They drew two fundamental conclusions: firstly, that community-based programmes increase parental confidence and competence and, secondly, that when planned and delivered in a participatory and restorative manner, family support has a more positive impact on parents than if the programmes were delivered in a 'top-down' style. This not only shows that the relationship between professional and service user within family support is central (as we discuss in chapter 8) but also that the participation of families in the planning of service delivery is crucial in empowering families to define their own needs and to understand how those needs can be addressed through partnership approaches.

Research undertaken by Putti and Brady in relation to a community family support service in the Republic of Ireland showed that there was a significant disparity between the views of service users and those of service providers, not only as to what constituted family support but also which services were perceived as being beneficial to families. There is a growing policy shift recognizing that, in order to deliver a needs-led and partnership approach to community family support, potential service users need to be central to the development of service design and delivery (Putti and Brady 2011: 272).

Given the definitional issues with family support and the fact that it can be delivered at different levels, there are differing expectations of what the service encompasses which can lead to frustration and a lack of consistency of vision and service delivery. Therefore, the gathering of potential users' views on services can from inception provide a needs-led direction to family support services in the community.

As well as highlighting the divergence in perceptions of need, 92 per cent of the Putti and Brady study's participants stated that services should be 'liberal or universal', with only 8 per cent favouring a more targeted approach to service delivery (Putti and Brady 2011: 277). These findings are crucial when considering policy shifts towards more targeted approaches, such as the 2010–2015 British coalition government's 'Troubled Families' agenda (see chapter 7 of this book). There is much evidence to suggest that families prefer services to be universal, non-stigmatizing and flexible and that when families are consulted on how they perceive their needs could be met, there is a greater chance of successful outcomes for families.

Children's centres provide an important example of universal, community-based family support. Children's centres are designed to provide neighbourhood-based family support through a continuum of preventative services, from primary services, such as playgroups and nurseries, to tertiary services, such as substance use and domestic violence programmes. Children's centres can encompass the full spectrum of services to meet and adapt to the needs of families within the community. Schedule Two of Part Three of the Children Act makes specific reference to 'family centres' being part of a range of services delivered under Section 17 (Department of Health 1989). Family centres received a boost following the implementation of the Act in 1991. In the United Kingdom context, the Sure Start programme, led by the New Labour government elected in 1997, progressed from local 'pram-pushing' distance projects to a universal and comprehensive provision of Sure Start community-based children's centres. This flowering proved to be short-lived following the 'austerity' cuts initiated by the coalition government from 2010 onwards. In Wales, there is a stronger emphasis on children's centres through the Integrated Children's Centres (ICCs), where the Welsh government requires 'all local authorities to operate a "team around the family" approach with a focus on early intervention to contribute to alleviating poverty for the most vulnerable' (Action for Children 2012).

The original intentions of the Children Act 1989 were to bring needs and family support to the centre stage. The Sure Start initiative advanced this further by concentrating on the interfaces of disadvantage, child development and family life. The Sure Start policy was designed within a wider remit to tackle social exclusion, recognizing the impact of economic disadvantage on family life, and sought to address the growing messages of the research literature that repeatedly drew links between poverty and adverse child development (Smith 1999).

## Child welfare under New Labour

The British New Labour government (1997–2010) introduced a variety of initiatives and policies aimed at supporting children and families: this added up to an attempted remodelling of British childhood. These ambitious initiatives included the introduction of Working Tax Credit, Child Tax Credit, the National Childcare Strategy and the Child Trust Fund (Millar and Ridge 2002). Perhaps most significantly, the Sure Start Local Programmes (SSLP), which developed into Sure Start Children's Centres (SSCC), embodied the strategy of giving universal access to services in every community, and it can be argued that it was around 2006 during the New Labour government that the emphasis on family support peaked. Evidence of this can be seen in the development of the Children's Trusts, Local Safeguarding Children Boards, and the overarching introduction of the *Every Child Matters: Change for Children* programme (Department for Education and Skills 2004b) which illustrated the ambition to improve outcomes for all children and put an emphasis on positive child welfare through the later-devised term *progressive universalism* (see Frost and Parton 2009 for a discussion of this).

This policy direction was conceptually focused on challenging social exclusion and centred on childhood as a crucial target of state intervention.

Child welfare was a decisive factor in promoting both economic growth and individual well-being (Frost and Parton 2009: 27). However, what also became apparent was that towards the end of New Labour's period in power, there was a growing body of critique relating to their childhood programmes. Parton, for example, asserts that the focus was no longer the 'tragic deaths of young children and the failures of professionals to intervene, but that many of the changes introduced may have had the unintended consequence of making the situation worse' (Parton 2012: 869). Changes such as the new Integrated Children's System, electronic records system and the Contact Point database became the subject of considerable academic and practice-based critique. Centrally, the emphasis on audit, measurement and inspection culture of New Labour left a damaging footprint on child welfare policy and practice (Garrett 2009).

## Sure Start: from local to universal coverage

The Sure Start Local Programmes were initially introduced in 1998 as a result of the Cross-Departmental Review of Provision for Young Children, which concluded that young children in the United Kingdom who resided in 'disadvantaged' areas were not receiving the appropriate support they needed. The review called for greater investment in the early years of a child's life. Sure Start were local programmes originally implemented to improve the health and well-being of pre-school children in deprived and disadvantaged areas, which relied upon the effectiveness of early intervention research, often originating in the United States (Duch 2005).

During 1999–2003, 524 Sure Start Local Programmes (SSLPs) were implemented in targeted disadvantaged areas, with local authorities, primary care trusts, local communities and voluntary organizations usually responsible for their development and implementation. SSLPs were established over a two-year period between 2006 and 2008. Sure Start was developed to encompass all areas of the country, and the New Labour government then committed to a national 'roll-out' of Sure Start Local Programmes which evolved into Sure Start Children's Centres (SSCCs), and children's centres were implemented in every community, rather than just the previously targeted disadvantaged areas (HM Treasury 2004), marking a significant shift from the previous strategy of targeted service delivery.

The evolution from SSLP to SSCC clearly illustrates the change in the policy direction at the time, and the previous mantra of tackling social exclusion had developed into a progressive approach that intended to encompass all sectors and groups of the community, and with that children's centres established themselves as a representation of the change from targeted services to progressive universalism. From the family Centres' focus on *support* to Sure Start's focus on *inclusion*; children's centres had 'added a third theme of *integrated services*' (Sheppard, Macdonald and Welbourne 2007: 62) [emphasis added].

The strategy of SSCCs was to provide a way in which families could access a variety of services from a team of multi-agency professionals in health and family support, claiming that this 'joined-up' service delivery would have positive outcomes for children and families in every community. The different elements of service delivery varied, depending on location, but the typical service provision included:

- parent and toddler groups;
- parenting courses and support;
- employment and training for parents;
- groups for teenage parents;
- groups for fathers;
- outreach family support;
- in-depth family support;
- breastfeeding peer groups;
- home-visiting support;
- speech and language development;
- impact evaluation issues;
- antenatal services;
- health-visiting services;
- counselling. (Lloyd and Harrington 2012)

As apparent from this extensive list, SSCCs were designed to operate within local communities, delivering a variety of flexible, person-centred packages of support based on a wide range of needs for children and families, aimed at eventually improving the life outcomes through the early development of children. However, as various evaluative research highlights, Sure Start Children's Centres were less effective than intended at addressing the needs of vulnerable children and families.

## The national evaluation of Sure Start

Sure Start, as often with family support practice as a whole, has struggled to provide evidence of a positive impact. The family and child functioning evidence after three years of Sure Start, as compared with areas without Sure Start, showed little significant change, with some indication that it has had an adverse effect on some of the most disadvantaged families (Rutter 2006: 135). These findings are extensively reported in the various outputs of the well-funded and ambitious National Evaluation of Sure Start (known as NESS – see www.ness.bbk.ac.uk). Equally, there has been an acknowledgement that there can be many explanations for the less than desirable outcomes sometimes reported in the research. In part, this is due to the difficulty in establishing and demonstrating effectiveness within a short timescale, but also to the very rapid pace of change for SSCCs which created major difficulties for local authorities and their delivery partners (Lewis, Cuthbert and Sarre 2011: 48).

## Children's centres

The 2010–2015 coalition government stated that 'we will take Sure Start back to its original purpose of early intervention, increase its focus on the neediest of families, and better involve organizations with a track record of supporting families' (HM Government 2010), thus highlighting the coalition government's agenda to target services and reduce provision as part of a larger fiscal strategy.

Just as the original move to place children's centres in every community represented the progressive universalism of the political climate at the time, their ring-fenced funding now being removed equally represents the current regression to targeted services, and symbolizes the political agenda of reducing state expenditure and targeting the families that are most 'troubling' for the pursestrings of the economy. This runs contrary to much longitudinal evidence indicating that this type of strategy has very little long-term benefit in the context of an austere economic climate, as discussed in chapter 2.

## Shifts in policy direction

When examining the current political agenda for children's centres and early help resources, it is clear that the coalition agenda diverges from centrally promoting this type of support. In January 2013, the *Guardian* newspaper reported that more than 400 SSCCs had closed in 2010 during the first two years of the British coalition government, with over half those that are still open no longer providing any on-site childcare. There is a clear danger of an emphasis on 'localism' and its resultant 'postcode lottery', particularly in an environment of austerity. Despite claims by the British prime minister, David Cameron, before the 2010 general election that he 'backed' Sure Start, the Opposition Labour Party stated that £430m had been cut from English local authority Sure Start budgets between 2010–11 and 2012–13 (Butler 2013).

The '4 Children' charity published a census in July 2012 detailing that, of 500 Sure Start Children's Centres examined, 55 per cent of them had removed on-site child care, a fifth had reduced the number of situated qualified teachers, a further fifth reported they would have to reduce childcare staff and a fifth were charging for services that were previously free.

However, the same report concluded that, in the face of significant reductions in public expenditure, many local authorities tried to secure levels of Sure Start funding, and children's centres were 'a picture of resilience and creativity' (4 Children 2012), illustrating that, despite significant budget cuts, local authorities still perceive the value and importance of protecting children's centres.

Some of the other changes that have occurred since the 2010–2015 British coalition government's reforms of children's centres have included: incentivized performance via payment by results; the introduction of charging families for services; the reduction of qualified staff; and a push for an increase in volunteers. These changes clearly mirror a stringent, targeted approach that fundamentally challenges the original intentions and visions of the service.

The introduction of payment by results for children's centres is troubling: incentivizing in order to further improvements and delivery presents a huge challenge for the children centre providers from the measurement of impact to the assigning of the prizes. In the face of the ever-dangling golden carrot, questions still remain about how success will be evidenced, how long-term preventative benefits will be measured and how funding will be split between income and rewards.

It is evident that moving to a more targeted approach, accompanied by dwindling budgets and expected increases in results, poses a very significant challenge for children's centres. The Children's Centre Census found that 75 per cent of managers felt that this new approach presented some of the greatest challenges for the future (4 Children 2012).

## Case Study: Sheffield Children's Centre

*Exercise*
Consider the qualities of the case study outlined below. Could you include any aspect of this study in your practice?

*Background*

> The rewards are immense. In a centre of this kind you can't remain in a gap; our lines find each other and our work inevitably overlaps because of the nature of the children's and the family's needs. It is a sense of community, that none of us is alone. Often people will help you to help others and it is this gentleness which is most rewarding for me and to see the fight going back into people who have been stamped on. (Maggie [pseudonym], Sheffield Children's Centre founder member)

Sheffield Children's Centre is a worldwide renowned community cooperative that has been running for over twenty years in a socio-economically deprived area of inner-city Sheffield, United Kingdom. It prides itself on having delivered and run these services long before the government's implementation of 'children's centres' as a nationwide initiative. Recognized for its advanced approach and good practice model, the centre has been successful through its ethos of community cohesion, common aspirations and principles, rather than through policy-driven initiatives. Broadhead, Meleady and Delgado (2008) comment that the centre is 'not an island, it is connected to a wider community' and that the explicit principles of the centre of 'equity and parity' cannot be divorced from the economic disparity and socio-political context (2008: 2).

Interestingly, the Sheffield Children's Centre challenges even the Sure Start initiatives through its undertaking of family support. The intentions of Sure Start were to improve prosperity for all community members; however, as Broadhead et al. comment, this may not account for the 'already disenfranchised', those people who are raised in communities where adults operate both beyond the economic mainstream and outside the dominant principles of existing childcare services (Broadhead et al. 2008: 7). The Centre's culture is characterized by the celebration of diversity, lifestyles and life choices and is successfully reaching those who find themselves on the fringes of society, unable to move within the confines of tidy packages of 'mums and tots' groups.

In essence, the organization enacts an opposing attitude to the 'social exclusion' and 'targeted services' agenda. Instead, it advocates on behalf of the marginalized and oppressed, mobilizing an ethos and core value base that readdresses the government's responsibility to recognize and act to limit the impact of poverty on the people that walk through the doors of the centre. Based on the work of Paulo Freire (1974), the centre confronts preconceptions of oppression, focuses less on goals such as parents returning to work, and more on families making the right choices for themselves in the face of considerable adversity.

### Account from Chi [pseudonym], an Early Years worker:

we might get called upon to help in a family's domestic situation; we try to refer across in the service but sometimes we have to do what's needed because the family will only want us because they have a relationship or trust with us. Often we are an access point for families . . . We do have to do court reports and go to court on child protection cases. We also do home visits and help parents with behaviour or play skills or just share and co-work with them for the benefit of the child. Visiting homes can put people at ease as it's more comfortable and they've got more control. We can work better between the centre and home in a partnership approach especially on concerning issues. (Broadhead et al. 2008: 12)

### Family account: The Oubi [pseudonym] family

I had a nervous breakdown after my husband ran away with my two children. He took them to his country of birth on a contact visit. The children had gone to the centre from being little. The centre helped me with legal advice and put me in touch with women like me. Because the staff are from different cultures and the centre works with different countries, they were able to make contact with the right people. And they located my children for me. Staff went over to bring my children back with the support of the government there. And they counselled me and my children throughout the process. We are strong; we are one again. Words cannot express how much we have benefited; only the angels know. Each day I wake up and see my children's faces and hear their voices in our home. It's a benefit only a mother would know. (Broadhead et al. 2008: 33)

*Case analysis*

From these two powerful illustrations, it is clear that the level of impact that family support can have is beyond the confines of statistical outcomes. It is apparent that part of Sheffield Children's Centre's practice is to be diverse in every way, provide culturally relevant services, remain flexible and family-centred and put the heart of the child and the families' voices at the centre of its work by continuing to adapt to the needs of the community. Family support aims to empower people, to offer a vehicle for change in the lives of those that are not integrated into society and are marginalized as a consequence.

The Sheffield Children's Centre prides itself on not conforming to shifts in policy directions and agendas and has managed to remain autonomous in its delivery. Its 'project identity' is a crucial component of its success, and it manages to encompass the characteristics of a family support identity, remaining politically opposed to disadvantage and culturally diverse and receptive to the needs of the local community. As illustrated by the two accounts, the centre remains flexible and committed to the families it serves. It operates outside of structural remits and professional jurisdiction, encompassing a wide range of professionals with a shared ethos of doing whatever it takes to support families to make the changes they see necessary in their own lives. Furthermore, the centre crucially manages to carry out elements of statutory work with social workers whilst maintaining relationships with families, successfully moving through the various levels of prevention while still managing risk.

## Conclusion

Having examined the literature surrounding children's centres' aims and ethos, along with one example of good practice in community family support, there are some core values and characteristics that resurface throughout which are worth considering when reflecting on the project identity of good community family support as delivered in practice. This is by no means an exhaustive list:

- spectrum of primary to quaternary support;
- strength-based approach;
- service-user consultation and involvement in service design and delivery;
- promotion of self-efficacy;
- encouragement and promotion of links to systemic networks, both formally and informally;
- cultural diversity relevant to the needs of the demographic;
- intrinsic awareness of wider disadvantage and offering resistance to oppression;
- flexibility and adaptability;
- participation;
- relationship-based practice;
- absence of stigma.

Community-based projects have their roots in the original ethos of family support. Using local systemic networks, mobilizing informal support and partnering with families in order to provide a wide range of support from universal to quaternary services is seen as essential. As shown in the case study, at times the project identity must attempt to remain consistent even in the face of adversity and austerity, using available local resources to advocate on behalf of families against the effects of disadvantage. Community-based support is as unique and varied as the communities it serves, but the values it holds must remain in keeping with the original intentions of family support and not pander to the changing political agenda.

> **Point for reflection:** Reflect on the advantages and disadvantages of a universal approach to the provision of children's centres.

### Selected further reading

Broadhead, P., Meleady, C. and Delgado, M. (2008) *Children, Families and Communities, Creating and Sustaining Integrated Services.* Maidenhead: Open University Press. This book draws on the excellent work of Sheffield Children's Centre, a renowned community cooperative, which is known worldwide for its progressive approach and good practice models that have emerged from true community participation. The text gives a coherent and accurate insight into the challenges and barriers to effective integrated community work, drawing on case study analysis as well as the wider themes of political context, upholding the moral legitimacy of family support with a tangible case study.

Freire, P. (1974) *Education: The Practice of Freedom.* London: Writers and Readers Collective. This work, much like Freire's other texts, seeks to redefine conventional interpretations and considerations of objectivity and subjectivity. Freire proposes that, because human beings are in the world, they must in turn integrate meaningfully with society. The book confronts global oppression head on, theorizing the importance of community living, cohesion and integration with compelling arguments that are very relevant to the role of proactive community support.

Parton, N. (ed.) (1997) *Child Protection and Family Support: Tensions, Contradictions and Possibilities.* London: Routledge. The contributors to this text create an encompassing backdrop to the continued tensions of support versus intervention. This text offers a refreshing intellectual and research-driven overview of the political and moral imperative to respond to messages from research as opposed to rare and reactive incidents derived from serious case reviews, all the while contributing to the wider argument for family support.

# 5 Home Visiting: A Key Process in Providing Family Support

There are many techniques and methods in the family support 'tool kit', a number of which are explored in this book. Such variety is indeed a major strength of family support. Perhaps the predominant technique, however, is the 'home visit': 'Home visiting programs operate under the belief that parents mediate changes for their children. . . . Home visiting programs also share a focus on prevention, be it prevention of low birth-weight babies, child abuse, reliance on public assistance, learning delays, and so on' (Sweet and Appelbaum 2004: 1435).

The diverse and optimistic nature of home visiting is illustrated by the quote above. The home-visiting approach is consistent with the advocacy of family support in this book as a child welfare practice which should be expanded and indeed comprehensively offered to families facing social problems. It can be employed at all four levels of prevention identified in the Hardiker Model, although it is predominantly found at the secondary and tertiary level.

Home visiting has been subject to a large body of research in the United States which we explore in this chapter, although it is perhaps under-theorized and reflected upon only fleetingly in family support training and policy development. Until recent work by Harry Ferguson (2011), the actual dynamic and detail of the home visit has been under-researched.

> **Point for reflection:** Think of a home visit you have undertaken. What challenges did you face in undertaking the visit?

## The home visit: some reflections

The implementation of home visiting was central to the origins of modern welfare practice. Historians often identify the introduction of systematic and recorded home visits as being initiated by the Charity Organization Society (COS). The early days of the COS are brilliantly analysed by Gareth Stedman Jones in his classic study *Outcast London* (1976). Formed in London in 1869, the COS was concerned about the indiscriminate giving of 'alms' (charitable giving): a similar movement developed in the United States about the same time (Charity Organization Society 1883). The COS pioneers felt that charitable giving would encourage laziness, fecklessness and vice. Rather than this indiscriminate approach, charity should be 'organized' so that it rewarded hard work and morality. This form of support would work by being personalized by the relationship between the home visitor and the household: the recipients should be encouraged and incentivized to improve their behaviour through this relationship. It is apparent that these themes of fecklessness and the deserving and undeserving poor are present in contemporary debates about welfare benefits.

It followed for the COS that if their strategy was successful, the home visitor would require training and should record their visits in order to encourage a systematic and organized approach. It is relatively straightforward to see the origins of modern social work here (Payne 2014).

The basic 'home visiting' model was developed by the COS and the early Societies for the Prevention of Cruelty to Children (SPCCs). The SPCCs started in New York, United States, in the 1870s and were soon exported to Liverpool, England, which formed its own SPCC in 1884. The purpose of the Societies was clear – to reduce and prevent cruelty to children – and, whilst a number of approaches were available (court proceedings, imprisonment of cruel parents, removal of children and public education, for example), the home visit was perhaps the crown jewel of the NSPCC approach. Inspectors were asked to undertake this process. In contrast to the COS, where the home visit was the domain of largely middle-class women, the NSPCC mainly employed formerly military men. They often covered large swathes of the country, on horseback if necessary, to undertake home visits. They would check the physical and moral welfare of children and offer advice, warnings and assistance as required. They would ask neighbours to keep an eye on children where this was feasible (Ferguson 2004).

In this brief historical review of home visiting, we have uncovered the core tension within it: to what degree are home visits a form of social control with which we may associate words such as 'monitoring', 'surveillance', 'control' and 'intrusion'? In contrast, is the home visit a form of support with which we may associate words such as 'help', 'support', 'assistance' and 'aid'? Perhaps in reality the threat of 'social control' sits behind the 'helping' offer of family support. This is the tension at the heart of home visits across the globe in everyday practice. It is a tension that informs the remainder of this chapter and which we will explore in our conclusion.

### The home visit: some key research findings

In this section, we draw extensively on two reviews of home visiting research undertaken in the United States. Sweet and Appelbaum (2004) and Howard and Brooks-Gunn (2009) conducted comprehensive reviews of family support home-visiting research which informs our discussion. Howard and Brooks-Gunn attempt to define home visiting. They point out the diversity inherent in the practice of home visiting:

> Home-visiting programs come in many shapes and sizes. Because home visiting is a method of service delivery and not necessarily a theoretical approach, individual programs can differ dramatically. They vary with

respect to the age of the child, the risk of status of the family, the range of services offered, the intensity of the home visits, and the content of the curriculum that is used in the program. (Howard and Brooks-Gunn 2009: 120)

Sweet and Appelbaum make a comparable point:

> Home visiting is an umbrella term that implies a strategy for delivering a service, rather than a type of intervention, per se. Programs differ along many dimensions, including the types of families served (e.g., single, teenage mothers; families of particular ethnicities; socioeconomic backgrounds; or social risk factors), targeted behaviours or outcomes (e.g., child abuse, school readiness, or mothers' employment), type of service delivery staff (e.g., nurses, or mothers from the community), ages of children targeted (e.g., enrolling pregnant mothers, or families with preschool children, length and intensity of services, types of services provided, methods of recruitment, and methods of assigning families to treatment groups. (Sweet and Appelbaum 2004: 1436)

We can see that home visiting is varied and difficult to define, a diversity making it very complex to research and evaluate. It could indeed be argued that there is no such thing as the 'home visit' but rather a range of home-visiting methods, with a variety of features and techniques being used. Howard and Brooks-Gunn believe, however, that there is underlying optimism that home visiting has a 'positive impact' and can improve parenting practice and therefore outcomes for children and young people (2009: 120). In the other research review we are exploring, Sweet and Appelbaum make a comparable claim that there is indeed a connecting thread that supports home visiting as a concept:

> Home visiting programs are linked by their method of service delivery, their goal of helping children by helping the parents of those children, and their focus on younger children. The method of delivering the service or intervention to families in their own homes offers advantages that parents do not have to arrange transportation, child care, or time off from work. Bringing the intervention into their home also provides opportunity for more whole-family involvement, personalized service, individual attention, and rapport building. These factors may aid families in and of themselves but may also increase program retention rates. (Sweet and Appelbaum 2004: 1435)

In other words, there is a shared belief across a range of studies and programmes in the efficacy of the home visit. This is based on a 'commonsense' technique, albeit one that, according to Ferguson (2004), is under-theorized: the technique fundamentally involves crossing the threshold into the family home. This raises many issues about the privacy of the family and the role of the state and philanthropic agencies, and the relationship between them (Frost 2011).

Whilst this basic 'crossing of the threshold' defines home visiting, according to Howard and Brooks-Gunn:

> The specific roles that home visitors play also vary quite a bit – and often fall in several domains. In some cases, the visitor is meant to be a source of social support; in other cases, home-visiting staff act as resource

> providers, linking families to social supports and providing them with referrals to other resources in the community, such as mental health or domestic violence services. Home visitors also often act as literacy teachers, parenting coaches, role models, and experts on topics related to parent and child health and well-being. Nurse home visitors, particularly, provide information to encourage healthy pregnancy, infant care, and family planning. (Howard and Brooks-Gunn 2009: 12)

Here we can see the multiple roles of the home visitor and the diversity of purposes: it is a method united by technique but varied in its aims. The stated aims of home visiting programmes, their length and intensity, vary from organization to organization. Sweet and Appelbaum collated the features of the programmes they investigated, as illustrated in the box below.

---

### The Nature of Home Visiting Programs

Primary Goals: Primary goals were the stated objectives or overall mission of each program. Up to four primary goals were coded for each program. The two most frequently reported primary goals were parent education (96.7 percent) and child development (85 percent). Parent educating goals included improvement of parenting skills, behaviors and attitudes, and parent–child interaction skills.

Populations Targeted: A small percentage of programs (6.7 percent) universally enrolled families. The majority of programs targeted families at some type of environmental risk (75 percent).

Intended Length of Program: Most programs were intended to last for 9 to 12 months (18.3 percent), 12 to 24 months (30 percent), or 24 to 26 months (23.8 percent). Some programs were intended to last for shorter periods (8.3 percent 0 to 3 months, 8.3 percent 3 to 6 months).

Home Visiting Staff: Programs listed up to three staff types that worked directly with families in their homes: professionals, paraprofessionals, and nonprofessionals. Most programs (75 percent) employed professionals, those with formal training and education before their home visiting work. Paraprofessionals, who often came from the same community as those being visited and were often helped by home visiting programs themselves, were employed by 45 percent of programs. A small number of programs employed nonprofessionals (8.3 percent) who had formal education but no home visiting training before employment.

*Source*: Sweet and Appelbaum 2004: 1437–8

---

This diversity of approach and intention provides many problems for research and evaluation programmes. Howard and Brooks-Gunn say that evaluation is essential to understanding the impact of home visiting but this is dependent on certain conditions: 'Developing more precise measures for assessing child maltreatment, using professional staff whose credentials are consistent with program goals, intervening prenatally with at-risk populations, and carrying out the programs with fidelity to their the-oretical models will make it possible to evaluate home-visiting programs more adequately so that their promise can be fully realized' (Howard and Brooks-Gunn 2009: 137).

Having explored what we understand by the home visit and having noted the variation in programme design and delivery, we now move on to ask: What does research tell us about the effectiveness and outcomes of this wide range of home-visiting techniques? One often avowed purpose of the home visit is to reduce the incidence of child abuse and neglect. In relation to this, Howard and Brooks-Gunn contend that '[a]lthough home visiting is commonly thought of as a strategy to help prevent child abuse and neglect, few programs actually measure child maltreatment as an outcome and even fewer are able to document significant effects' (2009: 121).

Another aim is to improve the home environment and parenting style and ability. In this context, Howard and Brooks-Gunn claim that the impact of home visiting has more 'positive effects in parenting domains than in child outcomes' (2009: 131). In addition, they argue that '[h]ome visiting programs are often associated with parental gains in responsivity and sensitivity in their interactions with their children' (2009: 131).

The home visit is inevitably associated with mothering, as opposed to a focus on the role of the father. Where home visiting is aimed at moth-ers, Howard and Brooks-Gunn consider that 'it is worth noting that some programs did identify small effects on stress and depressive symptoms and that others have specifically targeted reducing maternal depressive symp-toms and have obtained stronger results' (2009: 139).

With reference to mothers, Sweet and Appelbaum note, in something of a contrast to the argument above, that:

> [t]he more indirect measures of parent mediation of child improvement, the enhanced maternal life-course outcomes, were not as influenced by home visitation. Mothers in home-visited groups did not go back to school or seek out some form of education more than did control group mothers, but did not differ from control group mothers in terms of employment and self-sufficiency or reliance on public assistance. (Sweet and Appelbaum 2004: 1445)

The positive impact of home visiting on mothers is therefore lacking a strong evidential base. More particularly, home visiting is often aimed specifically at young mothers. Howard and Brooks-Gunn claim that there is evidence that home visiting has focused on teenage mothers. This is very important, they argue, because 'these women provide the true test of primary prevention program' (2009: 137).

One of the many consideration of home-visiting programmes is whether the visit is undertaken by volunteers, by para-professionals (such as family support workers) or by trained professionals, such as social workers and nurses (see Howard and Brooks-Gunn 2009: 135). This remains a contro-versial issue with mixed findings.

Howard and Brooks-Gunn make the case that efficacy rests largely on the planned nature of programmes: 'Analyses investigating whether the effectiveness of programs is more closely linked to the number of planned visits or to the number of visits that take place have shown that programs with more planned visits tend to be most effective' (2009: 137).

Having analysed and reviewed an extensive amount of home-visiting research, Howard and Brooks-Gunn provide limited and nuanced support for home visiting when they point out that, '[a]lthough findings are at best mixed with respect to the effectiveness of home-visiting programs in preventing child neglect, evidence is mounting that these programs can positively alter parenting practices and, to a lesser extent, children's cognitive development' (2009: 137). Further research-based support for home visiting is provided by the other research review we have consulted, where Sweet and Applebaum argue that '[i]t is also possible that home visiting programs do have real, practical use for some families, and that these families and their program experiences differ in some systematic way(s) from families who did not benefit from such programs' (2004: 1445).

The dominant research paradigm in terms of attempts to measure the impact of home visiting can be summarized as follows: it seems that home visiting does have a positive impact on families with young children, but Sweet and Applebaum contend that the cost effectiveness of this is not yet proven. They state that what exactly makes home visiting effective is unclear but:

> It is clear that home visiting programs can vary greatly along several dimensions, some of which may not be easily measured or even explained in program reports or evaluations. Some of those potential sources of variation are reasons for home visitation researchers to consider program standardization, both within individual programs and across the field. Standardization would likely enable future meta-analytic efforts to make more definitive statements about what types of programs work best for which types of outcomes. More definitive statements, in turn, might enable home visiting researchers to tailor their programs to meet better the needs of families enrolled. (Sweet and Applebaum 2004: 1446)

In their review, Sweet and Appelbaum reach the following conclusion, having reviewed a wide range of diverse home-visiting programmes:

> To be considered effective, home visiting programs must help both parents, the mediators of child enhancement, and children, the group thought to ultimately benefit from home visits. In general, children in families who were enrolled in home visiting programs fared better than did control group children. Within the set of child outcomes, three of the five average effect sizes were significantly greater than zero. Only child abuse and parent stress as an indicator of potential child abuse did not yield an average effect size of significantly greater than zero. (Sweet and Appelbaum 2004: 1445)

Having explored the complex and still formative findings on home visiting, it seems clear that home visiting does have a positive impact but that the nature and cause of this is difficult to pin down and define. Having explored these findings, we now provide a case study of a home visit.

## Case study: Home Visiting

*Exercise*

Consider the following case study. How effective is home visiting in this situation?

*Members of the household*

  Jerry – single father
  Jody – 9
  Mary – 7
  Robert – 4

*Background*

Jerry is a single father of three children, aged four, seven and nine. His wife recently died of cancer. Jerry is a caring father but is struggling to look after his children effectively. He is not managing to undertake all the necessary tasks: shopping, cooking, washing, ironing and so on are proving too much. He works 40 hours per week as a car repairer and gets some support with child care from a neighbour. The neighbour is worried that Jerry is stressed and grows angry with the children as a result. Jerry has no time for any hobbies or social life and is starting to feel lonely and isolated.

Jerry's neighbour contacted a voluntary home-visiting agency. The professional home visit organizer visited Jerry to undertake an assessment. An experienced male home visitor, Dave, was allocated to provide support.

Dave and Jerry formed an immediate bond: Jerry reports that Dave's visits are the highlights of his week. Dave visits twice a week but is flexible. He sometimes accompanies Jerry for the weekly shop whilst the neighbour cares for the children. They have a coffee and a chat in the supermarket cafe. Jerry finds it helpful to have someone to talk too and this helps him feel less stressed. Dave explains that everyone finds parenting hard and that he feels Jerry is coping well, particularly considering his bereavement. Dave has also been able to get some support for the children from a local charity that works with bereaved children.

The match between Jerry and Dave is working well. Jerry feels more cheerful and able to cope. He has an ambition to become a home visitor himself once the children are a bit older.

*Case analysis*

Whilst most home visits involve women visiting other women, this case study provides an example of the potential for home visiting in a range of situations. This is an example of the key role of home visiting at secondary level and shows how it can provide support to prevent situations deteriorating. It is also an example of support, rather than 'intervention', provided by organizations such as Home-Start. In this example, the home visitor is a volunteer and Jerry himself hopes to become such a volunteer in the future. In the Home-Start model, it is important that such volunteers have professional training, support and supervision (Frost et al. 1996: 200).

## Conclusion

We have argued that home visiting is an essential element of the family support repertoire, situated mainly at Levels Two and Three of the Hardiker Model. It is a straightforward principle: families in need of support are visited at home by professionals or volunteers (with professional support). We have seen that the type of model, intensity and duration of home-visiting programmes vary in their deployment. The research syntheses we have used find some evidence of positive outcomes from home visiting, but have some reservations. When recipients of home visits are asked for their own qualitative perspective on family support, these tend to be very positive (Frost et al. 1996). We have also uncovered a paradox in home visiting: is it a form of social control or a form of support? The reality is probably a mix of the two with a potential threat of social control lying behind the offer of support. Fundamentally, this book favours universalist approaches to welfare, rather than the United States model of a minimal welfare state supplemented by a range of programmes aimed at specific social groups. Research suggests a positive role for home-visiting programmes as part of a wider family support repertoire in keeping with the principles of family support we outlined earlier.

> **Point for reflection:** How convincing do you find the research on home visiting? Does it make a strong case for home visiting?

### Selected further reading

Howard, K. and Brooks-Gunn, J. (2009) The Role of Home-Visiting Programs in Preventing Child Abuse and Neglect. *Future of Children* 19(2) (Fall): 119–46.

Sweet, M. and Appelbaum, M. (2004) Is Home Visiting an Effective Strategy? A Meta-Analytic Review of Home Visiting Programs for Families with Young Children. *Child Development* 75(5): 1435–56.

These two literature reviews provide a comprehensive synopsis of home-visiting research. The diverse nature of home visiting is explored, as are the complex data on outcomes.

# 6 Parenting Education: A Universal or Targeted Service?

In recent years, there has been increasing emphasis on the responsibilities of adults, as good citizens, to contribute to the economy through employment and the responsibilities of parents to ensure the well-being of future citizens and thereby the health of society through good-quality parenting (Adams 2012). In this chapter, we will explore what is meant by 'good parenting' and discuss the proliferation of parenting education programmes aimed at promoting positive parenting practices. These programmes can be situated at any of the first three levels of the Hardiker Model. We discuss the policy developments underpinning current work with families in this area of practice and analyse the different approaches that have emerged to provide parenting education. Attention will be paid to the theoretical foundations of interventions to enhance parenting and what we can learn from research about effective parenting education programmes. We will conclude this section by considering a case scenario in which a parenting education approach may be applied in practice as an important element of the family support continuum.

> **Point for reflection:** What do we mean by 'parenting'? What are the features of 'good enough' parenting?

## Parenting and parenting education

Despite being common in everyday language, the notion of parenting is difficult to define: it is a socially constructed concept, whereby meaning changes across time and is culturally variable. The word denotes a relationship, a role, a process and a range of tasks. In essence, the verb 'to parent' refers to the positive activities undertaken by someone in a parenting role (usually the biological parent, but including significant others who may practise as primary carers) that facilitate the healthy development of the child from infancy through to adulthood. In contemporary discourse, the term is deliberately non-gender-specific, recognizing that both men and women are able to fulfil the role and tasks of parenting. Professional understanding of parenting in England has been shaped in recent years by the focus of the Assessment Framework on parenting capacity, which includes the following tasks or dimensions: basic care; ensuring safety; emotional warmth; stimulation; guidance and boundaries; and stability (Department of Health 2000: 21). This is an ecological approach which sets families within their wider social context.

It was Donald Winnicott (1965) who first coined the phrase 'good enough' parenting, recognizing that the role of providing a 'facilitating environment' for children to develop and reach their potential involves negative as well as positive impacts, ambivalence as well as satisfaction, for many parents. Winnicott's concept of good enough parenting has been influential in enabling child welfare professionals to consider their role in assessment and provision of family support to enable or enhance parenting capacity.

In recent years, it has also been increasingly recognized that parents are not necessarily 'naturally' endowed with the capacity, abilities, skills and inclination to fulfil the many and varied functions of parenthood from the moment of arrival of the first-born child. Parenting is a demanding and at times all-consuming role because babies and children do not arrive furnished with instruction manuals. The fragmented nature and complexity of contemporary family structure means that many of the challenges of parenthood are met by lone-parent or reconstituted families who lack the support of the extended family network (Ermisch and Murphy 2006), including the modelling, guidance and advice that has been the pattern for previous generations. The recognition that parenting is a learned behaviour and that skills may be taught, practised and acquired, has contributed to the recognition of the need for parenting education. A range of approaches has developed which focuses on improving the parenting skills of parents and carers, enhancing family relationships and preventing the development in their children of behavioural and emotional problems (Barrett 2010). Parenting education programmes have become established, often delivered through parenting groups set up in community-based universal services, alongside more targeted approaches. It is useful to examine the policy context for these developments within the United Kingdom.

## Policy framework for parenting education

As has been noted, the British New Labour government from 1997 brought to contemporary public policy a keen interest in family support, leading to an increase in service development. For the most part, the policy intention focused on valuing and supporting parents in their crucial role of protecting and promoting the welfare of the next generation. There was also recognition that some parents may need additional advice or education in order to undertake effectively the demands of the parenting task. As Sure Start Children's Centres (SSCCs) became established, initially in disadvantaged communities, one of the core services they developed was parenting groups aimed at providing support and education in an accessible and non-stigmatizing way. The growth of SSCCs across the country provided a forum for the development of parenting education programmes as a universal service available to any parent seeking to enhance their knowledge and skills.

New Labour policy was also concerned to reinforce parental responsibility so that parents would fulfil their role effectively, preventing the offending and anti-social behaviour that might otherwise be committed by their offspring. The Policy Research Bureau noted 'a period of intense policy focus on the interface between outcomes for children and inputs by parents' (Moran, Ghate and Merwe 2004: 13) which led to the introduction of parenting orders as part of the Crime and Disorder Act 1998, requiring parents of young offenders and persistent truants to attend parenting education programmes. This was the first time that parents had been required by public policy to receive education in order to fulfil to a satisfactory standard their very private role as parents, reducing criminality and improving the citizenship of the next generation.

The 2010–2015 coalition government continued the deployment of parenting education in the form of parenting orders. However, the so-called 'age of austerity' heralded the closure of some children's centres and a reduction in the numbers of parent groups. Waldegrave (2013) found that funding for children's centres has been reduced by 28 per cent since 2010, leading to fewer services and as a consequence a more targeted approach to the provision of parenting programmes.

A policy initiative was developed by the 2010–2015 coalition government, indicating that the interest of the state in parenting education remains active. After March 2012, a pilot scheme was developed whereby parents collect free vouchers from retail outlets or online and use them to purchase parenting classes provided by a network of voluntary organizations in their local communities (Cullen et al. 2014). The government has compared the parenting classes for parents of under-fives to antenatal classes, universal services attended by many as part of their preparation for parenthood. The then children's minister, Sarah Teather, commented: 'Parenting classes can be life-changing because they give parents the skills to manage challenging situations, give their children clear and firm boundaries and help them learn the consequences of their actions . . . The Government wants to make asking for parenting support the norm rather than the exception' (www.gov.uk).

An example is provided by the CANparent (an acronym for Classes and Advice Network) scheme which has been piloted in three communities, with short-term focused parenting education classes offered by established organizations such as the National Childbirth Trust or Save the Children. It is likely that private-sector, as well as third-sector, organizations will be encouraged to extend the service and the government is interested in the potential for this market to be developed, including through classes charging fees at the point of delivery. The CANparent Trial Evaluation (Cullen et al. 2014) has found that the concept of universal parenting classes has been welcomed by both parents and providers. This small-scale study found that almost all parents who completed the classes, the vast majority of whom were women, were satisfied with the course and would recommend it to others. The evaluation points to improvements in parenting skills and parents' well-being and supports the expansion of universal parenting classes. How, or indeed, whether this approach to parenting education remains a part of public policy remains to be seen.

> **Point for reflection:** Consider any parenting education you have been involved with in a professional role. What theoretical models or frameworks were useful in planning and undertaking the work with parents?

### Theoretical framework for parenting education

There is a wealth of literature focused on the examination of parenting styles and approaches, usually seeking to understand what are the qualities and skills of effective parents who succeed in the challenging task of raising contented children able to reach their full potential. Diane Baumrind (1967, 1989) is a key influential figure in parenting research whose work has led to the classification of parenting into three principal styles: authoritative, authoritarian and permissive. Work by Maccoby and Martin (1983) added a fourth parenting style: uninvolved or neglectful parenting. This model, based on the degree of parental responsiveness and sensitivity to the needs of the child, balanced with the level of parental expectation or

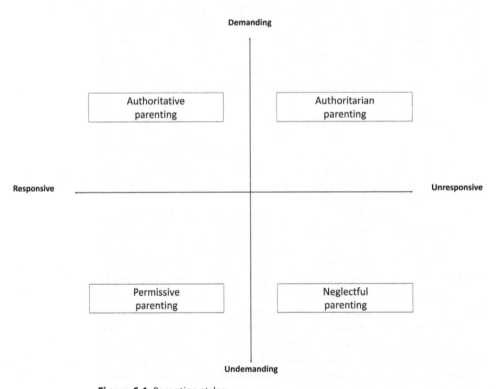

**Figure 6.1** Parenting styles

control of the behaviour of the child, has become influential in providing the theoretical foundation for parenting education.

A typology of parenting styles, which draws on the work of Baumrind (1967) and Maccoby and Martin (1983), can be outlined as follows:

- Authoritarian parents are demanding of their children, enforcing strict rules and lacking sensitivity and flexibility. Children may be obedient and academically proficient, but lack self-esteem and social competence, or be over-controlling and aggressive.
- Permissive parents may demonstrate warmth but be over-indulgent and set few limits or demands on their children. They are likely to raise children who struggle with authority, self-regulation and empathy for others.
- Uninvolved parents are neglectful of their children's needs and make few demands, being generally disengaged and unsupportive. Maccoby and Martin's study (1983) analysed adolescent development in areas such as psycho-social competence, school achievement and behaviour. They found that those with neglectful parents scored significantly lower in all these key areas, lacking self-control and self-esteem.
- Authoritative parents have clear rules and guidelines that they expect their children to follow, but respond to them with nurturance and warmth. They are assertive not restrictive, supportive not punitive. Baumrind's (1967) initial research with 100 pre-schoolchildren found that children of such families are more likely to be happy, socially competent and successful, with high levels of self-esteem and empathy.

There is a strong body of research to support this model. For example, Patterson's important study (Patterson, DeBaryshe and Ramsey 1989) highlighted the causal relationship between severe and inconsistent discipline, low parental interest and involvement and later conduct disorders in children. The publication that informed many modern developments around child safeguarding, 'Messages from Research' (Department of Health 1995), emphasized the devastating impact upon the emotional well-being of children of growing up in families characterized by 'low warmth and high criticism'. Research has repeatedly found that confident proactive parenting is associated with children having high self-esteem, positive social skills and school achievement.

Building on this evidence-based model, practitioners have sought to develop parenting education that enables participants to develop the knowledge and skills to become authoritative in their parenting style. A range of theoretical perspectives have come to inform and underpin the development of parenting programmes. In the United Kingdom currently, most parenting education is characterized by an integrated approach, influenced by cognitive, behavioural, humanistic and psycho-dynamic theories (Wolfendale and Einzig 2012).

## Practice developments in parenting education

In the 1980s, parent training programmes developed based mainly on behavioural concepts, focused on supporting parents of children with conduct disorders. Professional facilitators, often psychologists or health professionals working in clinical settings, trained parents in behaviour modification techniques, aimed at noticing, attending to and reinforcing positive behaviours, and using a range of strategies, in particular withdrawal of attention and stimulation, to limit negative or disruptive behaviours. As we have noted, the development of children's centres, usually offering parenting programmes as part of their range of targeted and universal services, has led to parenting education evolving from a community base and incorporating a wider range of theoretical perspectives.

It is useful to briefly examine some of the approaches that are widely in operation and that have dominated parenting education discourse.

- The Incredible Years Programme, developed and evaluated by Webster-Stratton and Taylor (2001), was originally delivered in the United States to groups of parents of children aged 0–8 years. The programme is based on cognitive and social learning approaches, focusing on positive parenting to enable children's development and manage behavioural difficulties. A range of methods includes video modelling, teaching behaviour and conflict management and, in some settings, separate 'Dinosaur' classes for children encompassing social, emotional and problem-solving skills.
- The Triple P, or the Positive Parenting Programme, was developed at the University of Queensland, Australia, as a system of parenting intervention that can be adapted and offered at different levels, dependent on the extent of need and the age and stage of the child's development (Sanders 1999). Central goals of Triple P are the development of parental confidence, self-efficacy and self-regulation. Cognitive and social learning theory underpin the process whereby participants are taught skills to manage their own behaviour and parenting practices and become independent problem-solvers. The classes focus on enabling parents to provide a positive learning environment and assertive discipline for their children, whilst also ensuring they have realistic expectations and take care of their own well-being.
- The Strengthening Families, Strengthening Communities (SFSC) programme was developed in the United States originally to support minority ethnic groups. It aims to improve parent–child relationships, promote positive discipline and increase community participation and healthy lifestyles (Steele et al. 2000). The programme includes exploration of how cultural and spiritual beliefs influence family life, values and approaches to child rearing. Knowledge of child development is taught and the programme is underpinned by social learning and ecological theories.

There is a growing consensus that skills and knowledge enabling effective parenting may be taught and that focused short-term groups provide a useful vehicle for learning (Lucas 2011). Nevertheless, concern has been expressed (Wolfendale and Einzig 2012) that discussions around the future development of parenting programmes may become polarized between advocates of open-access, universal approaches to parent education and those who favour a targeted approach, using behavioural models of parent training focused on reducing dysfunctional behaviour. Proponents of the universal approach are criticized for promoting costly services that are poorly evaluated: targeted approaches raise concerns due to their narrow goals and stigmatization of participants. In order to move forward from this perhaps unhelpful polarization, we think it more important to examine what works and how we can ensure that an appropriate range of services develop to meet the diverse needs of families, at the different levels of the Hardiker Model.

## What works: research findings

An initial review of the research in relation to parenting education may well lead one to conclude that this is an area of professional practice that has been more widely examined than any other and has consequently accumulated an extensive evidence base. There are certainly innumerable studies and evaluation reports that make expansive claims for the effectiveness of particular programmes for enhancing parenting skills and improving children's behaviour. However, increasingly, commentators are highlighting the need for caution in making sense of research findings. Helen Barrett's comprehensive review of a wide range of meta-analyses and systematic reviews of parenting programmes, carried out for the Family and Parenting Institute, found that many of the studies are of limited scale or are methodologically flawed; she draws the following conclusion: 'one consistent finding appears to be that parenting skills training programmes can have positive benefits' (2010: 2). However, Barrett also noted that much remains unknown about the mechanisms of the benefits: we know little about what works best for whom or why. Having stated that, many studies have sought to examine, rigorously and methodically, what might be learned from this relatively new and developing area of knowledge.

Barlow (1999) carried out a meta-analysis of 18 studies of parenting programmes focused on improving behaviour problems in children aged 3–10 years. Barlow concluded that group-based programmes were effective in reducing problem behaviour in children and that they were more effective than individual or family work. She also found that community-based programmes were more cost-effective and less stigmatizing for parents than clinic-based services. Webster-Stratton and Taylor (2001) reviewed a wide range of interventions focused on younger children aimed at reducing risk factors related to conduct disorder. They found that behavioural parent training consistently led to improvements in parenting practices and reductions in behaviour problems in children. They also emphasized that parent training, including attention to interpersonal and stressful issues impacting on parents, is more effective than programmes that ignore these factors.

There has been concern that exaggerated claims of some research studies have led to unrealistic expectations about the efficacy of parenting education programmes to address the complex needs of families at risk of child abuse. Child protection plans have regularly insisted on parents undertaking parenting skills courses in a 'one-size-fits-all' belief that attendance would ameliorate entrenched problems and safeguard children. In a high-profile English case, the realization that a mother, Tracy Connelly, conscientiously attended nine out of thirteen sessions of her local parenting skills programme prior to the untimely death of her son, Peter Connelly (Haringey Local Safeguarding Children Board 2009), has led to the recognition that parenting education may be a necessary, but rarely a sufficient, response to safeguarding issues.

Lundahl, Nimer and Parsons were interested in exploring the effectiveness of parenting programmes to strengthen safeguarding in families at risk of child abuse. They analysed twenty-three evaluation reports of targeted interventions. Whilst noting concerns about the methodological rigour of the reports, they recognized the value of parenting training programmes on the premise that:

> Parents will be less likely to abuse if they improve and expand their child-rearing skills, rely less on coercive child management strategies, and modify attitudes linked to harsh parenting. In addition many parent training programs include supplemental components designed to enhance parents' emotional wellbeing, such as anger and stress control, out of recognition that preventing child abuse is not simply accomplished through transmitting knowledge about child development and child management skills. (Lundahl, Nimer and Parsons 2006: 251)

Lundahl, Nimer and Parsons (2006) conclude that parenting education programmes which used a range of theoretical approaches and included behaviour management strategies impacted positively on parents' lives and had a beneficial role in changing perceptions about child behaviour and childcare practices. They noted that group training was more effective if it was combined with an individual element, recognizing the importance in complex cases of individualized programmes of intervention, developed collaboratively with parents, to address additional difficulties such as parental conflict or mental health problems and high levels of stress. This reinforces the importance of parenting education not being seen as a panacea in safeguarding cases but being, where appropriate, one part of a comprehensive family support and child protection plan.

Kane, Wood and Barlow (2007) carried out UK-based research aimed at collating the findings from qualitative studies of parenting programmes provided for parents of children with behaviour problems. From their review of studies, they found that, before engagement with the programmes, parents reported feelings of guilt for being 'not good enough' and anxiety from being out of control: they felt socially isolated and lacking in the knowledge and skills to manage their children's behaviour.

After completing the programmes, the following themes featured in parents' responses:

- feeling more in control and confident about their ability to cope;
- reduced guilt and shame;
- more empowered and able to seek support from other parents;
- greater understanding of children and competence in managing behaviour;
- increased ability to address their needs for support.

Lindsay, Strand and Davis (2011) carried out a comprehensive study to evaluate the effectiveness of three distinctive parenting programmes (Incredible Years, Triple P and Strengthening Families, Strengthening Communities) that had received funding from the government as part of the Parenting Early Intervention Pathfinder policy. More than one thousand parents completed pre-course and post-course measures, focusing on specific aspects of parenting and child behaviour. Most of the participants were mothers who initially reported low levels of mental well-being and efficacy as parents and the prevalence of substantial behaviour problems in at least one of their children. The research found significant improvements on all measures for each programme. The greatest impacts were around parenting style and well-being, with improvements also around parenting satisfaction and self-efficacy. There were smaller but nevertheless significant improvements in child behaviour. The SFSC programme was found to have lower effects across all measures, though it was noted that the aims and content of that programme were broader (including emphasis on cultural issues and community development), possibly explaining the difference in outcomes. The researchers acknowledged that some data were lost across all programmes due to a drop-out rate of approximately a quarter of parents, which they recognized as 'a common phenomenon in parenting programmes especially when participants, as here, are subject to socio-economic disadvantage and other adversities' (Lindsay et al. 2011: 11).

A number of themes have emerged from the research highlighting the limitations of parenting education programmes. One of these is the rate of drop-outs or, even more difficult to quantify, non-starters, indicating that this approach will never be effective or able to engage all parents. Another key theme is the gendered nature of parenting and the gender imbalance of attendance at parenting courses. Ghate, Shaw and Hazel (2000) have commented on the complex attitudinal and organizational factors impacting upon fathers' participation in parenting interventions. As family structures become increasingly diverse, there are particular challenges for all those involved in a parenting role in parenting education. Mockford and Barlow (2004) found that the parent who attended the classes, usually the mother, may be faced with difficulties implementing new strategies: the unintended consequences of attendance for some families included inconsistency of parenting style and increased parental tension. Nevertheless, in spite of the methodological concerns about research studies and the limitations of parenting education that have been highlighted, it is clear that there is evidence of effective practice. Research has demonstrated that parenting programmes have a significant impact upon: increasing parents' knowledge and skills; improving confidence and self-efficacy; facilitating peer support and consequently reducing children's behavioural problems.

## Case Study: Parenting Education

*Exercise*

Read the following case study and consider:

- How might a parenting education programme benefit this family?
- What should be the features of a parenting programme that would be helpful for the family in terms of aims, content and style of delivery?

*Members of the household*

> Janine – 22 – African Caribbean; mother of Jaz and 5 months pregnant
> Jaz – 4 – mixed parentage – son of Janine and Rashid

*Significant family members*

> Rashid – 30 – mixed parentage, Asian/British – father of Jaz
> Danny – 22 – white/British – father of the unborn child.

*Background*

Janine had a difficult childhood and spent some of her teenage years in and out of care. She has some contact with her mother but spends most of her time watching television with Jaz or visiting one or two friends who live nearby. She did not do well at school and has never worked but was keen to return to some form of education or training until she found out she was pregnant. Janine has ambivalent feelings about her pregnancy. She experienced post-natal depression after the birth of Jaz and is worried that this may occur again. She has a close bond with Jaz and says he is the best thing that ever happened to her. She acknowledges that Jaz 'rules the roost': she likes to let him have his own way to keep him happy.

Janine lived with Rashid from leaving care aged 17. Their relationship was volatile and, after several incidents of domestic violence, she managed to move away with Jaz and was rehoused in a flat of her own. Rashid now lives with his wife and baby, having Jaz to stay at his home overnight for contact once a fortnight. Rashid complains about Jaz's behaviour and says he needs a firm hand. Janine's relationship with Danny was short-lived. He is an old schoolfriend and lives nearby. He is keen to be involved in parenting the baby.

Jaz has commenced Reception class at the local school and his behaviour is causing concern. He is not toilet-trained, has little speech and is always on the move. He never attended nursery or playgroup and finds it hard to interact with other children; he tends to take things he wants from other children, sometimes pushing or biting them, and throws prolonged temper tantrums.

The class teacher has recently spoken to Janine about a parenting course that is due to commence at the children's centre attached to school.

*Case analysis*

There may be many benefits for Janine in attending a parenting education programme, which will create positive outcomes for Jaz and the new baby. As her own childhood was affected by upheaval and inconsistent care, Janine may lack positive role models and understanding about effective parenting. Her main aim seems to be to keep Jaz happy and that may have led her to adopt a permissive parenting style in the hope of enabling her son to have a happier childhood than her own. Her experience of post-natal depression, in the context of a volatile relationship, may also have meant she lacked the motivation or ability to develop a more authoritative parenting approach when Jaz was a baby. A range of factors has created a pattern of family life that has worked for Janine and Jaz to an extent but is likely to create difficulties for both of them as they cope with the transition to school and the arrival of a new baby.

Increased knowledge about child development will enhance Janine's understanding of Jaz's needs as he moves from infancy to this new stage of his childhood. The course may include input around parent–child interactions and daily routines, including toilet training, mealtimes and bedtimes, and behaviour management techniques to create safe boundaries within which children can explore and thrive. There may be opportunities for Janine to practice attentive play methods that she can use with Jaz to stimulate his ability to concentrate, settle and learn through interactive cooperative play. Development of a confident and supportive parenting style that provides attention which reinforces positive behaviour and sets appropriate limits around negative or anti-social behaviour will enable Janine to complement the work of teaching staff at Jaz's school, ensuring a consistent approach. There may also be 'added value' for Janine in attending the parenting programme at this time in that she will be able to establish a more effective parenting style when her baby arrives; she may also benefit from increased social support through new relationships with local parents and knowledge of the supportive services provided by the children's centre.

Significantly, the focus of this analysis has been upon Janine and her access, as a mother, to parenting education. This reinforces the notion that Janine, as a mother, is solely responsible for the effective parenting, or otherwise, of her children. Given her estrangement from Rashid, it is unlikely that he would attend a parenting class with his ex-partner. There is a concern, then, that new approaches adopted by Janine are undermined during Jaz's contacts with his father. Given Danny's expressed wish to be involved in the care of the new baby, participation in the parenting course might provide an opportunity for Janine and Danny to prepare for co-parenting. If this were achieved, it might have the further advantage of providing a protective factor against the impact of a possible episode of post-natal depression. The focus provided by the Strengthening Families, Strengthening Communities model might also be of value for Janine and her family by providing a focus on positive cultural identity and building deeper links within the local community.

In considering this case study, it is important to remember for Janine and Jaz, as for every family, that parenting does not occur in a vacuum. Whatever the benefits that might ensue from attendance at a community parents' group, parenting education cannot solve the social and economic problems that adversely affect families: poverty, ill health and unemployment. There are many challenges for parents seeking to build a safe and positive future for their children. Nevertheless, evidence suggests that parenting education is a useful family support intervention, enabling more confident parents to negotiate the complexities of family life and raise their children to thrive in contemporary society.

## Conclusion

We have seen that a topic as universal as parenting is amenable to family support approaches. Parenting has been theorized developing the very useful typology of authoritarian, permissive, uninvolved and authoritative parenting: the latter is the preferred model according to research. We have seen that there is positive evidence of the impact of parenting programmes but throughout this book we have argued for the universal availability of family support. This is certainly not the case when it comes to parenting education. The universal availability of parenting education might perhaps have a larger impact on the quality of family life than any other single initiative analysed in this book.

> **Point for reflection:** Think about your role as a parent, or how you were raised by your parents. Would parenting education have been helpful?

### Selected further reading

Barrett, H. (2010) *Delivery of Parenting Skills Training Programmes: Meta-Analytic Studies and Systematic Reviews of What Works Best.* London: Family and Parenting Institute. For students and practitioners with an interest in the evidence base underpinning practice, this text provides a comprehensive review of the research about parenting programmes.

Maccoby, E. E. and Martin, J. A. (1983) Socialisation in the Context of the Family, in E. M. Hetherington (ed.), *Handbook of Child Psychology 4.* New York: Wiley. This is a classic text in which Baumrind's classification of parenting styles is analysed and extended. It has been influential in providing the theoretical foundation for parenting education.

Wolfendale, S. and Einzig, H. (2012) *Parenting Education and Support: New Opportunities,* Oxford: Routledge. A collection of papers that provides an extensive overview of current thinking and practice in the area of parenting education and support and also highlights emerging ideas and directions in which practice could evolve.

# 7 Targeted Approaches: The 'Troubled Families' Initiative

As the post-economic crisis era turned into an 'age of austerity', certainly across Europe, universal welfare provision has been reduced. Part of this process has been to decrease provision at Level One of the Hardiker Model and move services upwards towards more targeted approaches. A research report published by the NSPCC entitled *In the Eye of the Storm: Britain's Forgotten Children and Families* (Reed 2012) examined the impact of the public expenditure restrictions on Britain's 'most vulnerable children'. Not surprisingly, the evidence showed that the most vulnerable children and families defined using seven categories, including worklessness, housing and low income, were most at risk in the adverse economic conditions following the 2008 financial crisis. The report showed that measures implemented to mitigate the effects of the recession are insufficient and the numbers of families in the vulnerable category are very likely to increase significantly over the coming years (Reed 2012).

The methodology for identifying the families living under the vulnerable definitions used a household data-set called the Families and Children Study (FACS):

1.  worklessness – no parent in the family is in work;
2.  housing – the family lives in poor-quality and/or overcrowded housing;
3.  qualifications – no parent in the family has any academic or vocational qualifications;
4.  mental health – the mother has mental health problems;
5.  illness/disability – at least one parent has a limiting long-standing illness, disability or infirmity;
6.  low income – the family has low income (below 60 per cent of the median);
7.  material deprivation – the family cannot afford a number of food and clothing items. (Reed 2012: 6)

The methodology for identifying vulnerable families by determining whether they have five or more of these characteristics is currently being used by the UK government for their 'Troubled Families' initiative (see Casey 2012 for a 'Troubled Families' report by the civil servant who was the architect of the scheme). The 'Troubled Families' initiative remains a contentious policy: one can see significant differences between the Munro report (2011b) and the 'Troubled Families' report (Casey 2012) – they are promoting differing approaches and using different language. The tone of the report from Louise Casey differs significantly from that adopted by Munro, as discussed in chapter 2 of this book. For example, Casey writes that 'The priority was to help families who were stuck with many problems, often responsible for causing problems, and also costing society a large amount of money in terms of the myriad of services that dealt with them without getting to the root causes; money spent simply containing families in dysfunction and hopelessness' (Casey 2012: 4). This illustrates a lack of clarity, unity and consistency within the coalition's children's agenda: perhaps hope in a shared view of child protection and the centrality of 'early help' is quashed quicker than Louise Casey can say 'parents need a wakeup call'! (Casey 2012: 3).

The impressive research report *In the Eye of the Storm*, drawing on work undertaken between 2003 and 2008, claims that the threshold used in the 'Troubled Families' report is 'entirely arbitrary' (Reed 2012: 7) . The research for *In the Eye of the Storm* examined families who have both fewer and more than five of the criteria outlined by the 'Troubled Families' initiative. It is argued that this gives a complete and more accurate portrayal of the vulnerability of poorer families. For example, the research that used slightly fewer measures challenged the misleading figure of '120,00 troubled families' (Casey 2012) and showed that there were more than three times as many families, 395,000, which had four or more vulnerabilities, 900,000 families had three or more, and 1.87 million had two or more such vulnerabilities.

The use of controversial data has been a tactic of political leaders to gain support for contested initiatives and programmes, the 'Troubled Families' initiative being no exception. Casey claims that 'troubled families' are costing the UK taxpayer some £9 billion per year (Casey 2012). Some researchers were publicly outraged by Casey's work. In an article published by the *Guardian*, Nick Bailey (2012), a lecturer in social and political science, maintains that it not only breached ethical guidelines but that:

> The report was portrayed as solid piece of research driving an evidence-based approach to policy making. Ministers ignored its own caveat in the report which said that the information [interviewees] gave us is not representative of the 120,000 families that are deemed as troubled and that if the report was meant to be a so-called 'dip-stick exercise', as it was described by the Department for Communities and Local Government, then why was it was given such extensive press and media prominence and why was it considered a reliable basis for policy? (Bailey 2012)

Recognizing the lack of credibility in research methods and the use of data is worrying when we consider the wide-scale support this initiative has received. Nonetheless, there are no doubt positives in addressing the vulnerability of families and the welfare of their children in a national initiative aimed to improve the conditions and lives of children. An evaluation of the Intensive Family Support Service (IFSS) in Wales reaches relatively positive conclusions:

Most of the families interviewed felt that the IFSS had been largely successful. In the majority of cases, families explained that a number of the issues they had faced such as substance misuse, acute mental health problems, problems with parenting, housing, gaining employment, children's truancy, and problematic/abusive relationships had been either fully or partly resolved following their engagement with IFSS. Similarly, most families described IFSS as a considerable improvement on the support they had previously received. (Thorn et al. 2014: 1)

However, silo-natured programmatic approaches with pay-by-results incentives for the local authorities are rarely as effective and beneficial to the families as they claim to be. Whilst programme-based initiatives which direct more spending to vulnerable families may bear some positive results, Reed (2012) believes that this does not compensate for the overall reductions in public spending. The 'Troubled Families' initiative illustrates that in reality 'early intervention' once again triumphs and leaves 'early help' succeeding in theory and policy rhetoric only.

In this chapter, we will examine targeted approaches developed to support families and improve outcomes for vulnerable children. We will analyse a range of issues concerning which families should be targeted in order to promote the welfare of children and young people. We will recognize the range of different approaches that have been developed over recent years, targeting different families or groups of children and based on various criteria or founded on particular theoretical or policy approaches. We will examine how theory and research informs practice in order to explore what we know about what works in the area of targeted family support. A case scenario will be used to illustrate a typical pattern of targeted intervention.

> **Point for reflection:** Why might government prefer targeted approaches to family support? Name one advantage and disadvantage of targeted approaches to family support.

## The impact of tax and benefit changes

*The Eye of the Storm* (Reed 2012) report simulates the impact of changes to the tax and benefit system between 2010 and 2015 in order to examine the effect on the most vulnerable families. The report found that the changes, on average, will have a negative impact on every type of vulnerable household analysed. The tax and benefit changes disproportionately hit the most vulnerable and that the negative impact on income will increase for the more vulnerable families.

The introduction of universal credit (UC) will result in an increase in income for some of the most vulnerable families but will not equal the losses resulting from changes to benefits such as housing and disability benefit. Combined with the public spending cuts, the research indicates that families with five or more vulnerabilities lose approximately £3,000 a year, a decrease in living standards of around 7 per cent. The government's introduction of measures such as targeted 'Troubled Families' funding and the childcare offer for two-year-olds does not compensate for the overall cuts in spending, which will amount to approximately £1,000–£2,400 per vulnerable family per year by the year 2015 (Reed 2012).

All this is significant when seen in conjuction with similar research which highlights and predicts the same problem: those children and families that are most vulnerable will be hit hardest by the combined cuts in public spending, benefit reforms and austerity measures (Browne 2012). This research predicts that relative child poverty is set to increase between the years of 2010 and 2016 by around 400,000 and absolute child poverty, as defined by in the Child Poverty Act 2010, will increase by 500,000. Both research reports (Browne 2012; Reed 2012) concur that vulnerable, low-income families with children lose more as a percentage than pensioners, those of working age without children and wealthier families. Even more central to this debate is that those families with younger children are set to 'slide into poverty at a critical stage' (Reed 2012). The impact of poverty risks undermining policies aimed at supporting families in foundation years, such as Allen's preferred programmes (see chapter 3) and the Family Nurse Partnership (FNP). This demonstrates that the debate about early intervention, family support and early help is not and cannot be exempt from the wider economic and social context. Both Browne and Reed call on government to urgently revise the local housing allowance and housing benefit cap, and they state that vulnerable families will be significantly worse off if urgent action is not taken to address these issues (Browne 2012; Reed 2012).

Universal services play an essential role in supporting families through times of stress and upheaval and do so without elaborate gatekeeping processes or potentially stigmatizing assessment criteria. However, many family support services have been developed on a targeted basis in order to manage (or ration) limited resources and respond to those deemed to be most in need.

> **Point for reflection:** Who are the children and families that support services should be targeting?

## Who are we targeting? Policy developments

Since the implementation of the Children Act 1989, one answer to this seemingly simple question is that the legal framework for professional practice points to children in need as the main target for assessment and intervention. These are the children defined under Section 17 as being most likely to experience 'impairment of their health and development' without the provision of supportive services. This is a wide group of children, including children with disabilities and those whose development may be impaired by the conditions they live in. The 'Children in Need' census, collated by the Department for Education, estimated that at 31 March 2013 the number of children in need in England was 378,600.

The New Labour government policy 'Every Child Matters' policy sought to target a wide range of vulnerable children: that is, those children who might otherwise fail to achieve the five key outcomes. During the New Labour period, these five outcomes became the mantra for all involved in child welfare at every level. These were: being healthy; staying safe; enjoying and achieving; making a positive contribution; and achieving economic well-being. The ambitious target to improve outcomes for every child was resourced partially by the provision of a universal network of children's centres. The New Labour philosophy, set out in their 'Supporting Families' consultation document of 1998, envisaged the expansion of universal services to support all families and the recognition of the need to reach out to and ensure inclusion of the most disadvantaged.

Alongside the development of the 'Every Child Matters' approach, the Social Exclusion Task Force was seeking to identify those families who required more targeted services because of the entrenched nature of the social problems they experienced. It was the Task Force analysis of 'Families at Risk' (2006) that starkly highlighted the negative outcomes predicted for the children of some multi-problem families and the economic burden these families imposed on the rest of society. Examples of these costs for children and costs for society include:

- children from the 5 per cent most disadvantaged households are more than 50 times more likely to have multiple problems at age 30 than those from the most advantaged 50 per cent of households;
- anti-social behaviour costs the public £3.4 billion a year.

The Task Force identified a set of risk factors that were particularly significant as indicators of disadvantage. These include:

- no parent in the family is in work;
- the family lives in poor-quality or overcrowded housing;
- no parent has any qualifications;
- the mother has mental health problems;
- at least one parent has a long-standing illness or disability;
- the family has low income (below 60 per cent of the median);
- the family cannot afford a number of food and clothing items.

It was estimated that approximately 120,000 families with children experienced five or more of these disadvantages and merited specific attention in order to reduce the negative impact for their children and wider society. The government made a commitment to roll out a national network of family intervention projects (known as FIPs), offering intensive support and specifically targeting families deemed to be high risk and involved in anti-social behaviour.

With the political priority being to reduce state expenditure in an 'age of austerity', the English 'Every Child Matters' policy was shelved. This stands in contrast to the situation in Scotland, for example, where the 'Getting it Right for Every Child' programme is a more developed and sophisticated version of 'Every Child Matters'. In England, the aim of the 2010–2015 coalition government was to target intensive family support interventions in order to bring about change for the families deemed to be most disadvantaged and most fiscally challenging for the public purse. We will go on to examine their 'Troubled Families' initiative in more depth.

## Who are we targeting? Practice developments

Alongside these policy developments, recent child welfare practice has been developed in order to target supportive services more effectively in order to meet the needs of vulnerable children. Practice developments have been informed by increasing access to research (for example, that commissioned and published by the Social Care Institute for Excellence) and also by the findings of various inquiries and serious case reviews. For example, the research led by Hedy Cleaver (1999) highlighted the often devastating impact on children of living with carers whose parenting is compromised by domestic violence, substance abuse and mental illness. These risk factors, often termed the 'toxic trio', have enabled professionals to recognize more clearly children at most serious risk and to target the resources of the multi-professional 'team around the child' (TAC). The collation of learning from serious case reviews, published on a biennial basis, has reinforced the importance of the 'toxic trio', the key risk factors impacting on parenting, as well as highlighting other factors relating to the vulnerability of the child that should not be ignored when targeting limited resources. Primarily, there is a recognition of the vulnerability of the very young: in the biennial review published in 2008, 47 per cent of the children who had been subject to a serious case review were under the age of one year, and two-thirds of the cases involved under-fives. Children with complex and multiple needs were also found to be vulnerable. The Biennial Review published in 2010 emphasized the neglect of adolescents and noted the increasing prevalence of young people involved in gang violence, self-harm and sexual exploitation. The dissemination of this knowledge has enabled services to be targeted more effectively to ensure that the most vulnerable children are not overlooked, perhaps at the expense of a wider focus on universal family support.

Other research has been useful in recognizing families who should receive targeted support. The work of the Baring Foundation stressed the importance of early intervention to support and enable the parenting skills of adults with learning difficulties who were caring for children. Significantly, Hedy Cleaver's updated research overview (2010) includes this recognition of the need to support the parenting capacity of learning-disabled parents. The needs of young carers, who may themselves be playing a supportive role with a vulnerable adult, have also been highlighted by research (for example, Dearden and Becker 2000) and has contributed to the development of specialist services. The learning from all these sources emphasizes the need for targeted services involving multidisciplinary workers and the coordination of the input of professionals from adults and children's services.

> **Point for reflection:** Consider any targeted family support you have been
> involved with in a professional role. What theoretical models or frameworks
> were useful in completing the assessment and planning the intervention?

## Theoretical frameworks for targeted approaches

The work of Brigid Daniel et al. (Daniel and Wassell 2002; Daniel et al.
2010) has provided a useful theoretical framework for application to the
assessment of and intervention with children and their families using targeted approaches. The resilience matrix that Daniel et al. have developed
draws on research to identify those factors that might generate positive or
negative outcomes for children. These are factors that are both intrinsic to
the particular child or young person – their individual resilience or vulnerability at this stage of their development – and those that are extrinsic
– encompassing the protective factors in their family or environment or the
adversity of their circumstances or experience.

The model emphasizes the need for a comprehensive and ecological
assessment, based on the Assessment Framework (Department of Health
2000). A targeted intervention should prioritize input that seeks to build
the resilience of the child, including participation in the process in order to
enable self-efficacy and enhance self-esteem. At the same time, the Child

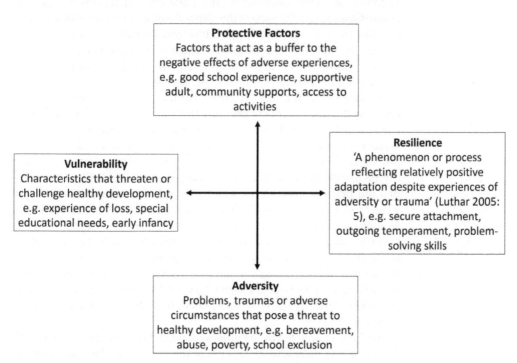

**Figure 7.1** The Resilience Matrix with summary definitions and examples (Daniel et al.
2010). Reproduced by permission of Jessica Kingsley Publishers

in Need or Child Protection plans should identify and address sources of adversity and strengthen protective factors, in particular recognizing the importance of a secure base and supportive relationships with caring, safe adults in the child's social network.

## Targeted approaches

Following an early help or comprehensive assessment and the development of Common Assessment Frameworks (CAFs), Child in Need or Child Protection plan professionals such as health visitors, learning mentors, child welfare and social workers seek to target family support services in order to safeguard and promote the welfare of vulnerable children. *Working Together to Safeguard Children* states that:

> Effective early help relies upon local agencies working together to:
> - identify children and families who would benefit from early help;
> - undertake an assessment of the need for early help; and
> - provide targeted early help services to address the assessed needs of a child and their family which focuses on activity to significantly improve the outcomes for the child. (HM Government 2013: 11).

Alongside this day-to-day work of child welfare professionals, in recent years a high-profile government initiative, the 'Troubled Families' programme, has been established. The initiative, led by director general Louise Casey under the wing of the Department for Communities and local government, was launched in 2011. It targets intensive resources in order to 'turn around' the lives of those identified as England's 120,000 most troubled families by 2015 (https://www.gov.uk/government/policies/helping-troubled-families-turn-their-lives-around).

The development of the 'Troubled Families' initiative has been influenced by the research of the previous government's Social Exclusion Task Force, which in its 2007 report noted the failure of supportive services to make a difference in the lives of families with complex and entrenched problems, describing an inadequate and uncoordinated response by a troupe of different welfare agencies and professionals. Louise Casey carried out her own limited research by interviewing sixteen families who were receiving help through family intervention projects (Casey 2012). As a result of interviewing 'troubled families', Casey expressed criticism of professional networks whom she felt provided inconsistent services, lacking the sufficient challenge and intensity to promote change. She concluded that the family intervention projects success lay in the importance of linking the family with a worker who would be 'dedicated, assertive and persistent' (2012: 3) and who would offer and coordinate intensive practical support.

The families targeted by the programme are those that have been identified as having entrenched, multiple problems that are having a severely damaging impact on the life chances of their children and are also causing problems for the wider community due to anti-social behaviour and by incurring high costs on public services. At the outset, in order to qualify for the 'Troubled Families' programme, the family had to meet three of the four following criteria:

- involvement in youth crime or anti-social behaviour;
- children who are regularly truanting or not in school ;
- an adult on out of work benefits;
- cause of high cost to the taxpayer.

The various features of the targeted 'Troubled Families' services are being developed by local authorities and delivered by a range of different providers. Nevertheless, they share the key criteria outlined above for access and are characterized by practical, intensive packages of support with a caseworker who is available outside regular hours to work alongside the family to model and teach parenting skills, such as getting children to school in the morning, developing bedtime routines and maintaining hygienic home conditions.

Some concern may be expressed that, besides being intensive, this approach to service provision is also extremely intrusive. The emphasis on assertive, authoritative intervention, often offered as a last chance prior to eviction, custodial sentencing or removal of children into the care system, runs contrary to value-based practice drawn up on the principles of empowerment. As 'payment by results' is a feature of this particular programme (Department for Communities and Local Government 2012), this also raises questions about the coercion of families to achieve specific targets that may not be *their* priorities, or even about how outcomes may be manipulated to ensure recompense. Furthermore, there are undoubtedly many other families beyond the targeted 120,000 whose children would benefit from a programme of intensive support but who do not fit the extremely prescriptive criteria. The emphasis on getting parents into the workplace has recently been criticized by Rhian Beynon, Head of Policy and Campaigns at the third-sector organization Family Action, who has noted that many barriers to employment exist for parents with mental health problems and that the main focus of the intervention should be the welfare of the child and supporting parenting. Nevertheless, there is no doubt that the provision of coordinated intensive support is providing a lifeline for some families and enabling more timely decisions to be taken about how best to safeguard the welfare of children. We will go on to look at the findings regarding what works in relation to targeted family support.

## What works: research findings

As was noted in chapter 3, research aimed at evaluating family support is often problematic, with difficulties around the assessment of the effectiveness of any particular intervention and how successful outcomes should be measured. In more targeted approaches, perhaps because the criteria for access to services is so specific and the aims of the intervention so focused, evidence collated through evaluation studies has drawn attention to significant and positive outcomes.

In Scotland, the Dundee Families Project, founded by Action for Children in 1995, has been seen as a particularly effective family support initiative and a forerunner of the family intervention projects and the current 'Troubled Families' programme. The evaluation by Glasgow University, published in 2001, carried out a review of 126 cases that had received intensive, targeted support from 1996 to 2000: focusing on 56 closed cases, it was found that nearly two-thirds of the cases (59 per cent) were recorded as having 'successful' outcomes, as all or the main goals had been achieved in these cases. The study concluded that the project offered good value for money and sustained gains for families in relation to:

- avoiding high-cost options (like children becoming looked after);
- reducing behaviours (including crime) with potential long-term cost implications for society;
- promoting the quality of life of family members. (Dillane et al. 2001: 18)

The evaluation study observed that key success factors were due to the nature of the intervention, which was intensive, integrated and flexible, and to the commitment of agencies and families to work together in partnership. A note of caution was sounded by the researchers in that 11 per cent of families did not engage in the project and the families' motivation for change was a key factor in the successful cases.

An evaluation of six family intervention projects in 2006 also highlighted significant successes. The report, written by Nixon et al. (2005), found that in more than 80 per cent of cases anti-social behaviour was significantly reduced and housing security (and consequently family stability) was greatly enhanced. These findings are reinforced by the statistics published by the Department for Communities and Local Government in December 2012, which emphasize that the national monitoring of family intervention projects across the United Kingdom from 2007 to 2012 has consistently gathered evidence of effective outcomes. They cite the following percentage reduction in family problems from referral to closure of cases:

- involvement in anti-social behaviour (59 per cent);
- involvement in crime (45 per cent);
- truancy/exclusion/bad behaviour at school (52 per cent);
- child protection issues (36 per cent);
- poor parenting (49 per cent);
- relationship/family breakdown (47 per cent);
- domestic violence (57 per cent);
- drug abuse (39 per cent);
- alcohol abuse (47 per cent);
- mental health issues (24 per cent);
- employment/training problems (14 per cent) (Department for Communities and Local Government 2012: 13).

The 'Troubled Families' initiative continues to be extended on the basis of such evidence and because of arguments in favour of the cost effectiveness of the interventions. The aforementioned government publication also concludes that there are five key factors that underpin effective targeted family intervention:

- a dedicated worker to provide flexible and coordinated input;
- intensive practical support;
- a persistent, assertive and challenging approach;
- an holistic assessment that considers the family as a whole;
- a sense of common purpose and agreed action between the professionals and the family.

The validity of some of the statistics cited in relation to these policy initiatives has been questioned. Gregg (2010) has expressed concern that family intervention projects did not select families who might have been difficult to work with. He also queries outcome measures based on opinion and self-evaluation, rather than on evidence of sustained behaviour change. In a December 2012 blog, written by Sue Kent of the British Association of Social Workers, concerns were expressed that the indicators of the success of the 'Troubled Families' programme were flawed and inaccurate. It is also clear that some of the targets are more difficult to attain than others. Whilst a parent being supported by a project to gain employment leads to that service provider gaining payment for this result, in a period of high unemployment, this target may be elusive, even more so for families where parents or children have complex needs or disabilities. It must be noted that, whilst securing a job may be easy to measure, the enhanced security of family life from the perspective of a vulnerable child may be a less tangible outcome. When considering evidence from evaluation studies, it is pertinent to bear in the mind the phrase adopted by Eileen Munro in her *Review of Child Protection*: 'Not everything that can be counted counts, and not everything that counts can be counted' (2011b: 45).

Nevertheless, the family intervention factors that have been defined by proponents of the 'Troubled Families' initiative as central to the effectiveness of targeted family support do chime with the findings of other researchers. The SCIE report of 2011, which focuses on interventions to support families where a parent has an enduring mental illness, emphasizes the value of targeted services based on holistic, whole-family assessment, with flexible intensive care planning coordinated by a skilful key worker. The study also notes the importance of taking an approach based on a strengths and resilience perspective that believes that change is possible and works to empower families through sharing information and ensuring active participation in the planning and delivery of every aspect of the work.

McKeown's (2000) influential summary of the research findings about what works in family support services for vulnerable children stresses the importance of the relationship between the key worker and the family in forging consensus about the nature of the targeted support and maintaining the commitment of all involved. This relationship factor seems to outweigh any prescriptions around the specific criteria for or method of intervention in terms of achieving positive outcomes. Significantly at this time of austerity, with increasing levels of family poverty, McKeown's text also includes an important reservation, noting that, more than any other factor, poverty threatens the achievement of proactive family support measures (McKeown 2000: 47).

## Case Study: Targeted Family Support

*Exercise*
Read the following case study and consider:

- What should be the targets for a family support plan?
- How should the key worker seek to engage all family members in the assessment and delivery of the plan?
- What changes would indicate the success of the targeted support plan?

*Members of the household*

Fiona Jones – 27 – white/British – mother of Hanif and Charlotte
Mick Smith – 36 – white/British – father of Callum and Charlotte
Hanif Khan – 7 – mixed parentage
Callum Smith – 12 – white/British
Charlotte Smith – 3 – white/British

*Significant family members*

Carol Jones – 50 – mother of Fiona – white/British
Nadir Khan – 28 – father of Hanif – Asian British
Jackie Smith – deceased – mother of Callum – white/British

*Background*
Fiona is divorced from Nadir and has been living with Mick for the last four years. Nadir has Hanif to stay at his home on alternate weekends. Fiona has a job at the local superstore but has been off sick for some months. Fiona suffers from chronic depression and has had some periods of in-patient care. On these occasions, Carol has stepped in to care for Charlotte and Hanif.

Mick's first wife, Jackie, died of cancer five years ago. Mick was made redundant last year. He is drinking at home and spends a lot of time in the pub. On one occasion recently, when he collected Charlotte from nursery, he seemed to be under the influence of alcohol.

Charlotte had been developing well and was seen by her parents as happy and lively. However, there has been a recent deterioration in Charlotte's health, she has lost muscle coordination and has been diagnosed as having Batten disease. The family are worried about what this diagnosis means for Charlotte's future. She attends the local children's centre nursery three days a week. Hanif gets on well with Charlotte and sometimes brings her to nursery in the mornings, which is next door to his primary school. Hanif has recently complained of being bullied at school and wants to change his name. Callum's behaviour is difficult at times. He regularly truants from school and has had two recent exclusions due to aggressive behaviour. He has been also recently received a warning for involvement in a 'joyriding' incident.

Fiona and Mick are finding it difficult to be consistent about managing the children and this is causing conflict. They are also struggling financially, debts are mounting and this is another source of tension between them. Recently when Fiona met with nursery staff about Charlotte's condition, she was seen to have a bruise around her eye. Fiona said she fell but there is concern about possible domestic violence.

The family live on a housing estate which is predominantly white/British. Fiona wants a housing transfer in order to be nearer to Carol but the housing office is not offering much hope of an early move.

*Case analysis*
It is clear from the multiplicity of complex needs that any plan for targeted family support would need to involve the input of a team of professionals, including staff from children's social services, children's centres, the youth offending service and mental health and substance misuse agencies. The importance of a key worker to coordinate the package of early help and to be the main source of support for the family cannot be underestimated. For this key worker to build relationships with the family members, seeking to engage the parents, including Nadir, and significant adults such as Carol, as well as listening to the children will be crucial to the ability to form some consensus and commitment to shared goals. Some incentives to work in partnership may be possible through access to priority rehousing. Challenge will also be part of the contract in order to motivate Mick to address his alcohol abuse. Research (Featherstone 2004) has highlighted the potential role of fathers as protective factors in the lives of their children. The resilience of the boys may be fostered by increasing Hanif's contact with Nadir and by working with Callum and Mick to develop shared interests. The flexible role of the key worker may afford opportunities to visit before school to improve household routines and to ensure that all the children get to school and nursery so that Hanif is relieved of inappropriate caring responsibilities. The establishment of employment which offers regular and flexible working patterns for Mick and Fiona, while enabling the level of care that the children will continue to require, might improve opportunities for the family. However, this may be extremely difficult to achieve. More confident parenting and more secure children are targets worth working for.

## Conclusion

Whilst recognizing the importance of universal services to enable accessible and non-stigmatizing support for all families as needed, it is clear that austerity measures and a shrinking public purse will probably mean that intensive supportive services are increasingly targeted to meet the needs of the few. It is crucial, then, that practice developments are based on a sound evidence base, rather than on any particular policy agenda, and that targeted interventions are able to effectively support children and families in need.

### Selected further reading

Cleaver, H. (2010) *Children's Needs, Parenting Capacity: Child Abuse, Parental Mental Illness, Learning Disability, Substance Misuse and Domestic Violence.* London: The Stationery Office. This text provides a comprehensive overview of recent research on the factors that impact negatively upon parenting capacity. This knowledge can inform effective assessments of the needs of children growing up in adverse circumstances. The publication is essential reading for practitioners, managers and policy makers concerned to ensure services are effectively targeted to improve outcomes for children.

Daniel, B. and Wassell, S. (2002) *Assessing and Promoting Resilience in Vulnerable Children.* London: Jessica Kingsley Publishers. Based on their research around resilience and protective factors, the authors have developed practical guidance for effective assessment and intervention in the lives of vulnerable children. There are three texts focused on work with children at different ages and stages of development.

Morris, K. (2013) Troubled Families: Vulnerable Families' Experiences of Multiple Service Use. *Child & Family Social Work* 18(2): 198–206. This article draws on a small-scale study examining the experiences of vulnerable families with complex and enduring needs. The perspectives of families on the receiving end of targeted interventions are analysed and insights gained about the processes that support or inhibit effective family support services.

# 8 Relationship-Based Family Support: An Underpinning Approach to Family Support

Effective family support work is usually predicated upon a positive professional relationship between worker and family: relationships matter across the full range of the Hardiker Model. In previous chapters, we have focused on methods of, or approaches to, intervention: implicit in much of this discussion is the importance of the relationship developed between the service provider and those accessing supportive services. In recent years, increasing attention has been given to developing understanding about the process of engagement and the skills needed by practitioners to establish effective supportive and enabling relationships with service users. A range of ideas has developed around relationship-based or reflective-relational practice (Folgheraiter 2003; Howe 1997; Ruch, Turney and Ward 2010) which recognizes the centrality of the practitioner–service user relationship. Theorists emphasize the responsibility of the professional to take a reflexive approach by acknowledging how their role, conduct and the quality of their interactions with service users impact upon the effectiveness of the supportive service they are seeking to provide. It is important that this applies to all parents and children, including fathers who can be excluded from child welfare services (see Maxwell et al. 2012 for a discussion about engaging fathers). In this chapter, we will analyse what we mean by relationship-based family support and how this approach has gained prominence in theory, policy and professional practice over recent years. We will examine how different kinds of research have been brought together to form an evidence base for practice, and we reflect upon a case study in order to explore the application of policy, theory and research in practice.

> **Point for reflection:** Consider a professional relationship you have been involved in as a user of a service. What made this professional relationship effective or ineffective?

## Relationship-based practice: the policy context

The *Framework for the Assessment of Children in Need and their Families* (Department of Health 2000) has provided the blueprint for developments in family support over recent years. In that policy document, there is reference to the importance of the childcare practitioner engaging in a positive working relationship with the family. The importance of inter-agency, multi-disciplinary assessment and intervention is emphasized, noting the need to avoid duplication by effective coordination of the Child in Need plan through the allocation of a professional with lead responsibility (section 1.23). The concept of 'partnership working' with families is seen as a key principle underpinning the assessment process, with professionals charged to develop a 'co-operative working relationship, so that parents or caregivers feel respected and informed' (section 1.44). Child centredness is another key principle that recognizes that effective assessment involves 'developing a relationship with children so that they can be enabled to express their thoughts, concerns and opinions' (section 3.42).

Following the implementation of the Children Act 2004, which extended the health and social care sector's understanding of and responsibility for child safeguarding, the role of the lead professional was similarly extended. The idea of the 'team around the child' (TAC) was developed to strengthen the notion of inter-agency accountability and cooperation: common assessments should be undertaken in order to address the needs of any vulnerable child, and the lead professional can be appointed from any section of the children's workforce (Children's Workforce Development Council 2009a). There is recognition of the importance of positive relationships and they are seen as a means to the end of enabling voluntary intervention, which is the basis for the common assessment process. Therefore, the role of the lead professional incorporates 'building a trusting relationship with the child and family (or other carers) to secure their involvement in the process' (Children's Workforce Development Council 2009b).

It can be argued that the concept of lead professional or key worker has remained largely a bureaucratic role – a means of ensuring agency accountability and coordinating interdisciplinary practice (Gilligan and Manby 2008; Pithouse 2006). Despite the positive notions outlined in the policies, in reality practitioners who take a lead in assessment or intervention processes have been limited by administrative demands with little time to build supportive or partnership relationships with children and their families. A feature of public policy affecting health and social care practitioners involved in family support has been the increasing bureaucracy impacting on every aspect of practice. In part, this is the legacy of New Labour's proliferation of targets and outcome measures related to the 'Every Child Matters' agenda, seeking to ensure compliance and accountability in the implementation of far-reaching government policy. This is coupled with the influence of new management developments adopted from the world of business and based on the assumption that efficiency can be improved through performance management strategies, including increased inspection and regulation. Furthermore, the media attention and public furore associated with high-profile tragedies, such as the cases of Victoria Climbié, Peter Connelly and Daniel Pelka, have led to a proliferation of procedures to ensure safe and risk-averse practice. Childcare organizations have sought to reassure the public that such tragedies cannot happen again because procedures have been improved and bad practice purged by rigorous monitoring. Commentators, such as Parton (2006) and Howe (1996), have emphasized that no amount of policies, guidelines or accountabilities can reduce the uncertainty and risk involved in managing complex childcare cases. The irony of this response has also been noted: 'Risk averse organizations whose business is working with people in need and distress often tackle their worries by building more elaborate systems that weigh practice down under a growing burden of rules, procedures, processes, targets and checks, all at the expense of the enterprise's humanity. As a result, safety decreases and danger rises' (Howe 2010).

The growing concern around this unintended consequence of recent public policy has led to renewed recognition of the importance of relationship-based practice. Bureaucratic practice that depersonalizes service users and turns practitioners into 'tick-box technocrats' has proved to be an inefficient and demoralizing approach to working with children and families. Eileen Munro, in her *Review of Child Protection* (2011a, 2011b), has been influential in challenging this malaise and re-emphasizing the importance of engaging with children and families and of involving service users as partners in the process of assessment and intervention. Munro recognizes that undue weight has been given to activities that are easy to measure and notes that managerial flowcharts fail to take account of the importance of the relationship between the practitioner and the family (2011b). She articulates the key principles of effective practice; primarily, that all work undertaken should be child-centred, involving an ongoing relationship between practitioner and child whereby children are listened to and enabled to participate in decisions about their lives (2.6). Also, she points out that 'helping children and families involves working with them and therefore the quality of the relationship between the child and family and professionals directly impacts on the effectiveness of help given' (Munro 2011b: 23).

Munro emphasizes an approach to working with parents that is supportive, compassionate and challenging: maintaining a focus on meeting the needs of the child, but seeking to engage parents in working together towards a shared goal. There remain questions about the implementation of Munro's principles in practice, particularly in an age of austerity leading to increased demands on limited public services. Nevertheless, her review has given impetus to relationship-based policy and practice.

> **Point for reflection:** Consider a professional relationship you have been involved in as a family support practitioner. What made this professional relationship effective? Were there any barriers to building a positive working alliance? How did you seek to overcome them?

## Relationship-based practice

In some sense, all family support work is relationship based. Whether the worker is intensively involved in providing the service or simply providing a contact point for coordinating a package of services, the work involves interpersonal communication and relationship building, even in the short term. This is acknowledged in the policy guidance and in the conceptualization of the lead professional role. However, this does not get to the heart of this emerging model of practice. Relationship-based practice involves practitioners engaging with service users in order to negotiate and sustain a supportive professional relationship in the context of challenging circumstances (Howe 1998).

Ruch (2005; Ruch, Turney and Ward 2010) has written widely on the subject, emphasizing the connections with psycho-social models and the importance of reflection. She sees the professional relationship as: 'the medium through which the practitioner can engage with the complexity of an individual's internal and external worlds and intervene' (Ruch 2005: 113). Such an approach to practice challenges reductionist understandings that perceive human behaviour as rational and logical, and complex problems as amenable to straightforward categorization in terms of cause and effect, vulnerability and risk, treatment and cure (Parton and O'Byrne 2000). Relationship-based practice recognizes the uniqueness of each service user and their particular circumstances, drawing on a diverse knowledge base, bringing reflexivity to the process of making sense of complexity and uncertainty (Ruch et al. 2010). It is perhaps not surprising that interest in this approach has developed alongside a critique of the kind of policy that has promoted procedurally driven administrative functions and has failed to adequately recognize or address the complex nature of social problems impacting on contemporary families.

Whilst forging good interpersonal relationships is desirable in most professions, it has been claimed that this is an absolute precondition for effective social work (O'Leary, Tsui and Ruch 2013); for this reason, discussion of relationship-based practice has been particularly prevalent in social work literature over recent years. No doubt, the discussion is relevant to the wide range of practitioners involved in family support work; however, it is pertinent to acknowledge that a relationship-based understanding of the role and function of social work is very much rooted in the origins of the profession. Social work developed through the last century from a casework tradition, rooted in psycho-dynamic theory whereby practitioners were mainly engaged in one-to-one work with clients. The casework relationship was central (Hollis 1964), with attention paid to emotions, repressed conflicts and subconscious processes in order to create change. Biestek (1961) outlined the principles of the emerging social work profession based around respect for the individual, being non-judgemental and building a relationship of trust and confidentiality. The profession moved away from these psycho-dynamic roots for a number of reasons, including the critique of individualistic approaches presented by commentators from Bailey and Brake (1975) to Thompson (1998) who maintained that the helping professions adopted expert status in order to pathologize the families they worked with, ignoring and at times perpetuating their experience of oppression. More recently, social work theory and practice has evolved to embrace structural understandings and empowerment approaches. Thompson's PCS model (1998) has emphasized the links between personal, cultural and structural levels of experience, providing a framework for practitioners to recognize and challenge oppression in each dimension. Commentators such as Fook (2002) and Smith (2008) have further focused attention on the power dynamics inherent in the worker–service user relationship. Assessing and intervening only at the individual level reinforces assumptions about personal inadequacy and responsibility, compounding for service users the sense of blame and making more likely responses of resistance which will hinder the development of a working alliance.

Contemporary understandings of relationship-based practice take account of the power relations inherent in the wider context of service users' lives and seek to challenge them (Smith 2008). This process starts with a negotiation of an effective, supportive and empowering relationship at the personal level. This involves recognizing the power relations that exist between the worker and service user, acknowledging the assumptions and beliefs about the status of the other and how these will need to be understood and negotiated in order to build a working relationship. Folgheraiter (2003) acknowledges that involvement of a helping professional tends to signify deficit and incapacity, but presents the opportunity for a practitioner to form a helping relationship, based on the service user's agency and self-efficacy. As Folgheraiter puts it: 'The surprise of a user when s/he feels accepted and respected as an actor – at the same time as his/her case is taken on because of his/her evident inability to be such – usually leads to the building and strengthening of a trust relationship, and therefore involvement in the helping relationship' (2003: 154).

As noted, this discussion about contemporary practice has tended to focus in particular on social work practice, perhaps understandably given the particular challenges for social workers of seeking to engage with the most vulnerable and marginalized families, often in the context of compulsory intervention. Nevertheless, developments in relationship-based practice have relevance for all involved in family support work. The practitioner–service user relationship in many forms of family support is the basis on which an understanding is reached about the needs of the family through the assessment process, and simultaneously the means by which the intervention is offered (Ruch 2005). Similarly, many of the challenges that exist for social workers in implementing this approach are equally pertinent for other childcare professionals.

When the Family Rights Group submitted evidence to the Munro review (2011) about the obstacles hindering engagement of families with safeguarding services, the issues highlighted by parents included:

- lack of clarity about the reasons for professional concern;
- confusion about agency processes;
- feeling under the spotlight of numerous different professionals;
- anxiety that they may have their children removed into care, making it hard to trust and work openly with professionals;

- the sense that decisions and actions are done *to* rather than *with* them, fuelling resentment and learned helplessness.

Many family support workers will recognize the prevalence of such hindrances, even in the context of voluntary supportive service provision. They underline the importance of the lead professional's commitment to the process of negotiating a trusting relationship by endeavouring to overcome such obstacles.

## Theoretical framework for relationship-based practice

As noted above, the roots of relationship-based practice lie in psycho-dynamic understandings of human development and interpersonal behaviour (Howe 1998). Although psycho-dynamic theory can be seen as being out of favour with practitioners involved in family support, many of the concepts developed by Freud and his successors have seeped into contemporary consciousness and influence our understanding of human relationships. For example, the recognition that our behaviours and choices are not always the outcome of rational thought but may be influenced by emotional or irrational subconscious forces, including reactions to past traumas, enhances professional understanding of complex patterns in the lives of service users and enables reflective practitioners to identify in themselves where such factors may be impacting on their professional relationships. Psycho-dynamic theory (Payne 2014) enables us to acknowledge that defence mechanisms that once served an adaptive purpose to protect our developing sense of self may be preventing alternative ways of being in the present; understanding that we can bring to our relationships with service users to make sense of processes of denial, repression, resistance and projection. Fundamentally, psycho-dynamic theory reminds us that seeking to understand the psychological factors that influence human behaviour, emotions and interpersonal relationships is important. Applying this knowledge reflectively enables practitioners to make sense of their own responses and reactions, to seek to manage their professional self in order to build positive working alliances with service users (Fook and Gardiner 2010).

Attachment theory grew out of psycho-dynamic understanding and reminds us how much relationships matter. According to Holmes (1997: 231), attachment theory is 'not so much a single theory as an overall framework for thinking about relationships'. The research of pioneers such as John Bowlby, James Robertson and Mary Ainsworth was based on the intensive and systematic study of parent–child relationships. They found that a range of attachment behavior is activated when young children feel insecure and need to gain the assurance, protection and proximity of their parent or primary carer. Separation or loss of the attachment figure led to unresolved distress, leading Bowlby (1979) to conclude that healthy child development was built on the foundation of a close, continuous caregiving relationship. Furthermore, physical presence coupled with psychological unavailability (carers who failed to respond adequately in order to provide comfort and safety) led to children having increased anxiety and insecure attachment patterns (Ainsworth et al. 1978). Therefore, within crucial early relationships, young children form internal working models of their own sense of self, security and worthiness, based on their carer's availability and responsiveness. 'So it is in relationships with other people that one learns to understand oneself. And by understanding one's self, one begins to understand other people. Thus the world of relationships is both the problem to be solved and the means to its solution' (Howe et al. 1999: 21).

Attachment theory is frequently applied in family support work, underpinning interventions to increase the trust and empathy between parent and child or to enhance the sensitivity and responsiveness of carers (Howe et al. 1999). Understanding attachment theory is also fundamental to recognizing the value of relationship-based family support practice. It acknowledges the potential for relationships to create change. Within each new relationship is the opportunity to alter internal working models and to challenge beliefs about the responsiveness of others and the worthiness of one's self. It teaches the importance of attachment styles, both in the practitioner and the service user, and that defensive strategies adopted in times of stress and anxiety are adaptive responses designed to establish security. Reflective practice can enable the worker to manage the intense emotions they may encounter in themselves and others when working in complex cases and to build self-awareness and resilience. Crittenden (2008) says that the child welfare worker may, in some cases, function as a kind of transitional attachment figure, developing a therapeutic alliance with parents and acting as a secure base. This may not be feasible or appropriate in every case, but for some families the empathetic presence of a trusted professional may provide a bridge which may enable change.

In line with this approach, another theoretical perspective emerging from psycho-dynamic roots that has influenced relationship-based models is person-centred practice. Focused specifically on the therapeutic process, Carl Rogers recognized that aspects of the relationship between therapist and client were fundamental to the potential for positive change. Rogers identified three essential characteristics, or core conditions, for the helping relationship: warmth, empathy and genuineness. This understanding continues to hold resonance for professionals involved in contemporary human services and forms the basis of ethical practice in many areas of work. Alongside the recognition that structural oppression must be challenged and the need for practical support addressed, the core conditions are fundamental to building an effective alliance and are a powerful component in family support work – one that is necessary, if not always sufficient. In this theoretical context, we can also return to the concept of child-centred practice. Lady Justice Butler-Sloss memorably reminded the professional community that 'the child is a person, not an object of concern' (1988: 245). Recognition of the rights of children, combined with an appreciation of children's capacity and agency and the importance of their

participation, has meant that person-centred theory has provided a foundation for developing an understanding of child-centred practice.

## What works: research findings?

Commentators who argue for the importance of relational approaches to
practice draw from a range of research sources in order to build their evidence base. McKeown (2000) notes the similarities between family support
work and therapeutic practice and cites the extensive literature that recognizes the importance of the relationship in practice. He claims that 'family
support can be, and usually is, a therapeutic intervention. Like all therapeutic interventions, its purpose is to help people – whether child, adolescent,
parent, couple or family – to overcome life problems by facilitating them to
make positive changes in themselves and their relationships' (2000: 10).

McKeown goes on to note that research about therapeutic interventions
has concluded that four factors influence effectiveness in the following
degrees:

- client characteristics and social support: personal and environmental
  factors intrinsic to the client that he/she brings to therapy – accounting
  for 40 per cent of therapy outcome;
- therapist–client relationship: the quality of the relationship based on
  factors such as the warmth, respect, empathy and genuineness demonstrated by the therapist – accounting for 30 per cent of outcome;
- client hopefulness: the degree to which the service user expects and is
  motivated towards change – 15 per cent;
- therapeutic technique: the approach or method employed by the practitioner in the intervention – 15 per cent. (McKeown 2000)

It can be seen, therefore, that the quality of the helping relationship has
twice the potency of any one strategy or theoretical technique in contributing to a positive outcome. Furthermore, Morrison (2007) has maintained
that the combination of understanding the needs and characteristics of
the service user within their social and environmental context via the
assessment process, combined with establishing a purposeful and attuned
relationship, accounts for 70 per cent of the potential for positive change.

However, there is evidence that at times the work of practitioners in
human services falls short of the standard required to build effective relationships, the kind likely to promote positive outcomes. Focusing on the
work of child protection social workers, a study carried out by Forrester
et al. (2008) found that there was a tendency at times for practitioners
to use communication styles lacking in active listening and empathy,
characterized instead by confrontational or aggressive inputs. A study of
parental participation in child protection processes (Ghaffar, Manby and
Race 2012) found that approximately 40 per cent of respondents felt that
they were not consulted or involved in decision-making processes, and
some parents experienced contact with professionals who lacked empathy
or were judgemental.

Studies of the implementation of the Common Assessment Framework (CAF), in which local family support workers took the role of lead professional in order to work with parents and children, found that workers had generally been able to engage with mothers, although they only recorded their views in half of the cases, and there was very little communication or engagement with fathers or children (Gilligan and Manby 2008; Pithouse 2006). Work carried out by the Office of the Children's Commissioner (2011), pertaining to the views of children and young people about involvement with social workers, found that 50 per cent of the 150 respondents felt that their key worker never or rarely took notice of their wishes and feelings. Some children reported that they only saw their social worker at meetings and that the worker did not listen or seem interested in their view of the situation. Nevertheless, this study also emphasized that young people highly valued their relationships with social workers where their relationships were positive; when they had trust in their social worker, children felt involved and able to have a say. Returning to the study carried out by Ghaffar et al. (2012), it was found that 76 per cent of the parents in their sample were able to identify one professional with whom they had a positive working relationship and that the support that they were offered was greatly valued by them.

There is a strong body of research into the views of service users and patients, built up over recent years, which echo these findings. Studies consistently show that the quality of the relationship with the helping professional matters significantly to service users, who value workers who are honest and direct, trustworthy and reliable, warm and empathetic, respectful and approachable (Beresford, Croft and Adshead 2008; Maiter, Palmer and Manji 2006). In stressful situations, such as where there are safeguarding concerns, de Boer and Coady found that families appreciate transparency and reciprocity in relationships with child welfare practitioners. They value 'soft, mindful and judicious use of power and humanistic attitude and style that stretches traditional professional ways-of-being' (de Boer and Coady 2007: 32). This reminds us that it is not the professional background of the worker that matters, nor necessarily what the worker does; it is how they do it that can make the difference. Being able to apply these traits and interpersonal skills in a consistent and supportive manner during crisis situations and despite the pressures of a heavy workload is what lays the foundation for effective relationship-based practice.

## Case Study: Relationship-Based Family Support

*Exercise*

What would be distinctive about relationship-based family support practice in this case?

*Members of the household*

Narinder – 30 – Asian/British – mother of three children
Nisha – 9 – Asian/ British

Amrit – 7 – Asian/British
Priya – 3 – Asian/British

*Significant family member*

Tariq – 35 – Asian/British – father of the children

*Background*
Narinder is a Sikh woman of Indian origin. She has a physical disability that has deteriorated over recent years. She struggles to leave the house due to poor mobility and extreme fatigue; she is unemployed and finances are tight. After the birth of her third child, her marriage became increasingly difficult. The arrival in this country of her husband's parents and their disapproval of Narinder, due to her disability, led to the breakdown of her marriage. Narinder's family live on the other side of the country and contact with her ex-husband is infrequent and unreliable. She feels lonely and isolated; she sees local organizations as Muslim and male-dominated; she feels alienated from her community due to her disability and her divorce. At times, she knows she is not coping; she shouts a lot and has smacked Amrit and Priya on occasion when she has lost control. Nisha is her mother's little helper; she provides support with household tasks and does most of the shopping. She takes Priya to nursery at the local children's centre on the way to school. The washing machine has recently broken down, placing more pressure on Nisha. Narinder feels that she needs support, but is anxious to seek it, fearing judgement from professionals, being seen as an inadequate mother due to her disability and possibly losing her children into care or to her husband's family.

*Case analysis*
It is important in this case for an early help assessment to be carried out and support to be offered before the family situation reaches crisis point. The lead professional role will be crucial in making a personal and professional connection with Narinder, offering reassurance that the aim will be to support the family and provide the help needed to enable the children to thrive in their mother's care. The lead professional may be appointed from the local children's centre, a Young Carer's Service or a similar agency, and may be from the same or different ethnic background as the family. What is more important than who the worker is or where they come from is *how* they work with the family. From a relationship-based perspective, the lead professional will seek to engage with Narinder and the children and to involve them in the process of assessment and intervention from the very first contact. This will involve listening to Narinder, seeking to understand her internal and external world; being open and honest whilst exploring together what might be the possibilities for the future; and developing a relationship based on the core conditions of warmth, empathy and genuineness. It will mean involving the children and finding age-appropriate ways of enabling them to express their views, wishes and feelings. If family

members demonstrate anxiety or a reluctance to engage, the worker should not simply withdraw and close the case or escalate the concerns due to a perceived unwillingness to address the risks on a voluntary basis. Reflecting on the many factors that may be affecting the family – from unconscious anxieties to media images intensifying fear of social care workers – and while examining their own assumptions and beliefs to ensure these are not creating obstacles in any way, the worker will take responsibility to reach out to Narinder and her family in a supportive and enabling way. Adopting an ethical approach to working in partnership, the lead professional needs to develop a plan for intervention, starting with priorities that matter to the family, seeking consensus in order to move forward, rather than imposing his/her own or agency targets. Recognizing that relationships matter, workers must look to build family and community support networks, enabling their own input to close at an appropriate point.

## Conclusion

There are clearly challenges inherent in relationship-based approaches to family support, particularly in terms of managing the demands of such practice in a context of decreasing resources and bureaucratic imperatives. There are also risks around the management of professional boundaries, including the need to focus on the welfare of the child and to maintain professional objectivity within a model that values connection with parents and the whole family. Nevertheless, there is a growing evidence base and policy impetus to apply the principles of reflective–relational approaches when working with children and families. According to Ruch (2005: 115), '[w]hilst challenging, the risks inherent in engaging in relationship-based practice appear to be worth taking if it leads to the well-being of children and their families being more sensitively and accurately understood and effectively responded to.'

### Selected further reading

De Boer, C. and Coady, N. (2007) Good Helping Relationships in Child Welfare: Learning from Stories of Success. *Child and Family Social Work* 12(1). This article reports on a small-scale study that analyses the qualities inherent in positive helping relationships by exploring the perceptions of workers and service users. The findings are of interest to family support practitioners and in particular to anyone involved in the training and supervision of child welfare workers.

Howe, D., Brandon, M., Hinings, D. and Schofield, G. (1999) *Attachment Theory, Child Maltreatment and Family Support*. Basingstoke: Palgrave. Although published some time ago, this book provides an excellent introduction to attachment theory and the importance of positive relationships both within the family and between professionals and family members. The discussion in the book emphasizes the value of family support interventions.

Ruch, G., Turney, D. and Ward, A. (2010) *Relationship-Based Social Work: Getting to the Heart of Practice.* London: Jessica Kingsley Press. With a focus on social work practice, this text is nevertheless of value to any family support professional with an interest in developing their understanding and skills in relationship-based practice.

# 9 Family Group Conferences: Involving and Empowering Families

Family group conferences (FGCs) provide a high-profile example of family support practice. The practice, which originated in New Zealand, has taken root across Northern America, Western Europe and Scandinavia, for example. FGCs in many ways represent the key principles of family support: listening to families, empowering them in relation to decision making and attempting to transfer power from professionals to the extended family network. FGCs sit within the restorative practice paradigm – the philosophy of 'working with' rather than 'doing to' the people you work with.

In this chapter, we explore the underpinning theory and practice of FGCs, research findings and policy and practice directions. (This chapter draws on Frost, Abram and Burgess 2013a and b).

> **Point for reflection:** Have you attended a family group conference? If so, reflect on the strengths and weaknesses of the process.

## Family group conferences: history and development

Family group conferences (FGCs) can provide the central plank of a family support platform. The Family Rights Group defines FGCs as follows: 'A decision-making, and planning process, whereby the wider family group makes plans and decisions for children and young people who have been identified either by the family or by service providers as being in need of a plan that will safeguard and promote their welfare' (Family Rights Group 1993). Connolly further defines the FGC process as follows: 'The Family Group Conference is a participatory model of decision making with families in child protection. It is a legal process that brings together the family, including the extended family, and the professionals in a family-led decision-making forum' (Connolly 2006: 90).

The FGC has four distinct stages. The first is the 'preparation stage' where an independent coordinator works with the extended family network to plan the FGC. The process includes exploring who should be invited to the FGC, the date, the time and the venue of the FGC and the nature of any refreshments to be provided. The coordinator spends time with family members, mediating and preparing them for the conference. The coordinator establishes that the focus of the FGC is on the best interest of the child or young person. The second stage is the 'information giving' stage which takes place at the beginning of the conference. Professionals share their concerns with the family and the family asks the professionals any questions that they may have. The third phase is 'private family time', where all the professionals, including the coordinator, leave the family on their own to produce a plan that attempts to address the professionals' concerns. The fourth phase involves the family sharing this plan with the professionals. Provided the plan does not leave the child 'at risk', the professionals are asked to agree to the plan.

Whilst the authors of this book support FGCs as a major element of a comprehensive family support approach, like other aspects of family support, FGCs exist in a complex relationship with the safeguarding system. This tension is a consistent theme of this book. As Mayer points out, FGCs 'address but are also constrained by paradoxes in the child protection system about commitments to protecting children and to family autonomy' (Mayer 2009: 10).

FGCs now have an extensive reach, in terms of geography and practice areas, being used in areas of practice including youth justice and leaving care, as well as in relation to children and young people in need or at risk. FGCs can be practised at Levels Two, Three and Four of the Hardiker Model. The research evidence on FGCs is extensive compared to many other aspects of family support, although there has been relatively little work on the actual outcomes, as Brown states: 'Despite the growing interest internationally in family group conferencing and the vast number of local evaluations that have taken place there still remains a dearth of rigorous research evidence concerning the outcomes for children of decisions made through the family group conference' (Brown 2003: 336).

The research evidence that exists on FGCs is rather mixed. There are studies that report positive outcomes (see, for example, Crampton and Jackson 2007; Pennell and Burford 2000). Other studies describe less optimistic outcomes (for example, Berzin et al. 2008; Sundell and Vinnerljung 2004). However, we note in the spirit of this book, and given our aspiration to focus on process (how we do things) as well as outcomes (the results of what we do), that process evidence for FGCs is very positive, suggesting they have a clear, empowering and supportive role. According to the research, participants feel listened to and appreciated, demonstrating some value to FGCs, even without definitive outcome evidence.

Whilst there is a need for long-term studies to examine whether FGCs can bring about sustainable change and produce positive outcomes for children, it is important to note that FGCs can provide an environment in which empowerment may occur; 'it is not an end in itself but an on-going process of collaboration and empowerment' (Pennell and Burford 2000). Process as well as outcome matters.

Family support campaign groups have supported and advocated the role of FGCs. For example, the Family Rights Group has consistently requested more extensive utilization of FGCs in the United Kingdom and, in 1999, the Department of Health promoted FGCs as a 'positive option for planning services for children and families' (Department of Health 2000: 78).

FGCs in the United States were initiated in the late 1980s, and became known as Family Group Decision Making (FGDM), a process which was supported by the American Humane Association (Brown 2003; Hoover 2005). Throughout the 1990s, FGC pilots were held in Australia, Canada, Sweden, Denmark and Israel. By 2005, it was estimated that some thirty countries had implemented the practice, including in areas such as youth justice, criminal justice and mental health (Nixon et al. 2005).

## The process of family group conferences

There exists a developing research base for FGCs. Lubin (2009) advocates the use of the FGC model for cases of child neglect in the United States. He considers that the most important difference between dominant models within the United States child protection system and FGC-based models is the role of decision making. This is because FGCs allow families a significant role in the actual decision-making process because the family network decides how it is going to address professional concerns rather than being the passive recipient of 'expert' professional decision making. By giving families this degree of control, FGCs allow private family time. Lubin suggests that this is where the particular strengths of the FGC process lie: in the FGC, family members are 'full participants in the decision-making process' (Lubin 2009: 134). This is consistent with the participative and empowering approach advocated by the authors of this book.

However, there has been some concern that private time may give abusive and powerful adults too much influence over proceedings (Biss 1995). In contrast, it can be claimed that disclosure about violence to the family network can increase support, as found in Connolly's (2006) study where an uncle was revealed as an abuser and the wider network took increased control over the situation. Similarly, it can be argued that if parents and carers help develop the plan, they are more likely to take ownership of it and comply with it.

In his evaluation of FGCs in New Zealand, Levine (2000) concluded that private family time was the most important element in empowering families. Research on FGCs reports that private time led to plans that professionals described as superior to those from traditional case conferences (Lupton and Stevens 1997) and also to greater family satisfaction (Pennell and Burford 2000). Levine (2000) suggests that if families can gain an empowering experience from FGCs, they may move on to address their own problems more effectively. Lubin believes that 'the adversarial system does not work for neglect proceedings; it places parents in a position where they feel inferior and reprimands them' (2009: 132). A strengths-based approach proposes that the reason for this is that parents do not believe that they are able to change their circumstances and this increases their feelings of helplessness. This was one of the Maori community's criticisms of the system in New Zealand before FGCs were established (Lupton and Nixon 1999).

Lupton, Barnard and Swall-Yarrington (1995) interviewed family members about their experience of FGCs and found that around half of them felt the information given by the professionals was useful or sufficient. They felt that reports were sometimes dominated by jargon: 'The information had no human side; it was all professional words' (family member, quoted in Lupton et al. 1995: 91). Family members also stated that they wanted to be able to ask questions while the social worker was going through their report but were told to wait until the end, by which point they had forgotten what they wanted to ask. If family members feel this way during the information-giving stage, they are less likely to be able to fully participate in making a plan and this is more likely to increase the power imbalances between professionals and families. The conduct of the information stage is crucial to the tone and nature of the FGC.

Levine (2000) discusses the challenges for professionals in adopting the more empowering role implied by FGCs. There are obvious concerns that professionals might use their status and authority to direct discussion and influence the family members and that FGCs cannot change the power balance. Ban and Swain (1994) notes that families may sometimes be coerced into outcomes preferred by the professionals. Some studies show that family members sometimes turn to professionals for direction (Lupton 1998; Maxwell and Morris 1992). This may suggest that the professional's role has not been fundamentally altered: he or she is still in an authoritative position, presenting as the holder of 'expert knowledge'. Hardin (1996) found that professionals wanted to listen in on the families' private time which, he claims, raises doubts about their commitment to changing the relationship. There was a general concern that professionals found it difficult to hand some of the power over to families and had problems fully adhering to the FGC philosophy (Lupton 1998; Lupton and Stevens 1997). This suggests that FGCs need to be part of a holistic commitment to an empowering, restorative process in a workforce development framework.

The FGC differs from the child protection conference (CPC) used in the United Kingdom in the existence of the role of independent coordinator. The coordinator aims to redress the power imbalance between professionals and the family by networking prior to the FGC. Marsh and Crow (1998) recommend that the coordinator should be well trained in the FGC process and have a good understanding of the principles underpinning it. In their studies, the authors found that the majority of coordinators came from a social work background. The role of coordinator is an essential element of the FGC (Frost with Elmer 2008). It is the coordinator's job to be independent and ensure that all parties have their views heard and respected. Some professionals can find it difficult to accept or understand their change of role and, if left unchecked, this can undermine the whole FGC process.

Marsh and Crow (1998) report a high level of parental and extended family participation at FGCs in comparison with the usual CPCs. Lupton and Nixon (1999) attribute this level of involvement in part to the work undertaken by the coordinator at the preparation stage. They believe that being clear about the need for an FGC, its aims, the people involved and the reason for their involvement is crucial to effective participation. Whilst the majority of family network members agree to FGCs, research shows that many are initially negative about the idea (Lupton et al. 1995). Lupton (1998) believes that most families will agree to an FGC because they are aware that other forms of intervention will be applied if they refuse, reflecting the ambivalent role of FGCs within the child welfare system. For family members to be effective participants, they need to have a clear understanding of everyone's roles in the FGC and know that they will be asked to come up with their own plan. This is a key responsibility of the coordinator.

A key element of the preparation stage is the mediation between family members. Marsh and Crow (1998) found that several family members said they would not attend if someone else, for example an ex-partner, attended. Marsh and Crow argue that it is the role of the coordinator to persuade family members to put aside their differences and to concentrate on the fact that the conference is about meeting the needs of the child, emphasizing that their common goal is the child's welfare. They cite successes in bringing family members together using this approach but warn that coordinators should be prepared to be persistent. present evidence that taking this approach can be positive; they find that family members who had been persuaded to let another family member be involved found that the problems they had expected did not materialize (Barker and Barker 1995: 5). Smith (1998) goes further, claiming that his interviews with family members demonstrated that the high level of family participation was appreciated by family members, in particular by the young people concerned. Other feedback from families suggests that the majority of family members that went to an FGC found the high degree of family participation a positive experience and felt that they were able to contribute actively to the meeting (Barker and Barker 1995; Lupton et al. 1995; Smith 1998).

For the conference to be successful, the family participants need to feel that they have the ability to come up with a plan and to believe that this plan will be valued and used by professionals; they need to feel that they have some decision-making power. If family members have had a previous disempowering experience of a child protection conference, they are likely to question why an FGC would be any different and why people would take notice of their ideas or their plan. The coordinator has two main jobs that require him or her to be trained in restorative-based family group conference approaches. Coordinators need to make it clear that they are independent and that their role during the conference is to ensure that both sides have their views heard and respected. The coordinator may need to spend time helping parents and other family members to see that they have strengths and resources that they can contribute and to believe that their contribution will make a difference. Barker and Barker's study (1995) found that the majority of family members were clear that the coordinator was independent of social services and child protection services. Rosen (1994) found evidence that all family members thought the preparation work was crucial to understanding the process and what they needed to focus on in the conference. Similarly, Lupton et al. (1995) in their report found that the majority of family members in a pilot study appreciated the independent nature of the coordinator's role. In all three studies, however, there were a small number of family members who did not seem to realize that the coordinator was independent of social services. The coordinator needs to have good communication skills and should ensure that all participants understand their role before proceeding to the conference. These studies reflect the inevitably different levels of skills possessed by coordinators which may be an important variable in studying the effectiveness of FGCs.

Another responsibility of the coordinator that is central to the FGC process is ensuring that the practical arrangements for the meeting, such as the time, day and venue, are in place. The coordinator consults the family before choosing an appropriate venue, time and date that maximizes attendance. Evenings and weekends may be opted for and professionals are asked to accommodate conferences at these times. This can cause difficulties with professionals who often work long hours and are unable to recoup this time. Feedback from family members in a range of studies (Barker and Barker 1995; Lupton et al. 1995; Rosen 1994; Smith 1998) showed that they were in favour of meetings being held in neutral venues, rather than in social services buildings, at times convenient to family members. Lupton et al. (1995: 95) quote a participant who felt that holding the meeting on neutral ground helped family members feel equal. Letting the family choose the venue can increase their sense of control and helps to redress the power imbalance. Marsh and Crow (1998) suggest that the coordinator should also organize refreshments, including food. This not only indicates that families are being looked after but also that the conference may be a long process. It also helps them relax and makes the meeting feel less formal (Lupton and Nixon 1999). This aspect of the conference reflects the origins of FGCs in the Maori community's tradition of collaborating over food.

The independent coordinators play many important roles in the FGC process. Much of a meeting's success can be attributed to a coordinator's skills in communicating, facilitating, mediating and so on. Marsh and Crow (1998) found that coordinators spent an average of 22 hours over two to four weeks setting up a single conference. Barbour suggests that the outcome of an FGC will be strongly influenced by the ability of the individual coordinator. She maintains that 'its heavy reliance on the strengths and commitments of the coordinators' is a potential weakness of the process' (Barbour 1991: 21).

Most of the relevant literature describes the process of the FGC and the experience of professionals, family members, children and young people, primarily using face-to-face interviews, along with some observational studies. Several pilot studies have been carried out in the United Kingdom (see Lupton and Nixon 1999; Marsh and Crow 1998). In the absence of a comparison group, this literature focuses on information gathered through interviews with participants of FGCs. This can give an insight into their experiences which can then be compared to those of traditional CPCs elsewhere in the literature. Marsh and Crow (1998) state that, overall, researchers report that family members are very positive about using the FGC model. Barker and Barker (1995) observed that family members found the process difficult and emotional but agreed that it was a natural way to make decisions and that they would choose to deal with future issues in a similar way. Marsh and Crow (1998) state that researchers did not ask interviewees to compare FGCs to the traditional CPC but found that family members nevertheless did compare the FGC favourably to other methods. Marsh and Crow conclude that participants are generally positive about the model and want it to continue.

Lupton and Nixon conclude that a large majority of the family members they interviewed felt they had been given the information they needed for the conference and were able to 'participate actively in the decision making process' (1999: 136). They also felt they were able to voice their views which were generally listened to and respected by other family members and professionals alike. The authors found that family members were particularly positive about the family private time and approved of holding the conference in a neutral setting. Lupton and Nixon (1999: 137) then compared this with the Thoburn, Wilding and Watson (2000) study on traditional CPCs which found that less than one-quarter of parents actually attended conferences and, of those, a third felt they were not listened to and nearly half felt their views did not carry any weight.

## The outcomes of family group conferences

As we have seen, there is quite an extensive literature on the process of undertaking FGCs and FGDMs but relatively few examine outcomes: in particular, there are few longitudinal studies which track change and outcomes over time. Weigensberg et al. reinforce the message about the limitations of the literature on the outcomes of FGCs as follows:

> Although there are a few studies that have contributed to the FGDM literature regarding child and family outcomes, there are several serious limitations to previous FGDM studies . . . Most prior studies evaluating FGDM outcomes were conducted in site-specific geographic locations with small sample sizes, contributing to the need for research using larger samples and samples that are more nationally representative. Also, most studies lack the ability to follow FGDM meeting participants over time, therefore limiting their ability to have follow-up data to assess outcomes after several years. (Weigensberg, Barth and Guo 2009: 384)

Whilst looking predominantly at the desired outcome, that of taking children out of the care system and keeping them in placements within the family, Crampton and Jackson (2007) analysed data from a Michigan study that compared 96 referrals that were served by FGDM with referrals that were served by mainstream care services. They recognize the weaknesses of their own study by acknowledging that it did not use randomized assignment to compare FGDMs with conventional services and that it therefore cannot prove or disprove the effectiveness of FGDM. However, their findings were that children placed through the FGDM programme were less likely to be placed in an institutional setting and more likely to remain with extended family. They moved less often between temporary homes and had less contact with the Child Protection Services (CPS), in particular less contact leading to substantiated claims of abuse or maltreatment.

In contrast to these positive findings, a Swedish study concluded that their data did not support the view that the FGC method is more effective than traditional models in preventing child maltreatment. In this Swedish study, Sundell and Vinnerljung (2004) compare 97 children served by an FGC with 142 children served by a more traditional child protection approach. They followed the children for three years and compared the two groups for future child maltreatment events reported to the CPS. After controlling for the children's age, gender, family background, and type and severity of problem, they found the FGC group had more re-referrals to the CPS (for abuse but not neglect) and they were longer in out-of-home placements but over time had less intrusive support from the CPS. The researchers note that the FGC group were often re-referred by their extended family, which might be the result of the FGC making the extended family more aware of the situation and therefore more alert for any further abuse. The researchers report that many proposed plans involved extensive and intrusive support from members of extended family, including reporting parents to social services if they revert to their former drug use. Sundell and Vinnerljung also emphasize that the impact of the FGC accounted for less than 7 per cent of the variation in the outcomes and, as such, demonstrated limited positive impact (in Crampton 2006: 205). Sundell and Vinnerljung report positive immediate process-based outcomes: FGCs had high family attendance (75 per cent of all extended family members invited and 67 per cent of all children invited). In all cases, families were able to agree on a plan and 65 out of 66 were immediately accepted by social services. In 86 per cent of the plans, members of the extended family offered some form of support and researchers found 72 examples of the issues addressed in plans had not initially been raised by professionals, the family having identified other issues themselves that they felt needed addressing. Furthermore, they reported high levels of participant satisfaction with regard to being well informed about the FGC, having their views listened to by everyone and being respected by professionals. At the end, 89 per cent were satisfied with the plan and 86 per cent favoured the FGC as a child protection method. Sundell and Vinnerljung conclude by stating that, although their results do not support the claim that FGCs are more effective, they do not disqualify their use. Again, we can see from this important study, one of the most rigorous quasi-experimental studies in the field, that process emerges more positively than outcomes. It is also noteworthy that increased scrutiny of families leads to increased awareness of child abuse incidents.

Crampton (2006) believes that the absence of FGDM projects in producing positive child welfare outcomes could possibly be accounted for by the failure to support families in the medium and short term after the conference. This points to the need for longitudinal studies of the outcomes of FGCs.

When comparing studies of FGC projects, one should be aware that the nature of FGCs may vary greatly from one project and cultural setting to another. Lupton and Nixon (1999) discuss concerns that the philosophy of FGC may become compromised when projects change aspects of the FGC policy and process. For example, in the Riverside, California project in the United States, the model used did not include private family time which is usually understood as one of the essential components of the FGC. Given the importance of all the different features of the conference, including the practical arrangements such as refreshments and venues, it is important to recognize that these may vary from study to study and, as such, might influence the effectiveness of the project. For example, Pennell and Burford (2000) explain how they decided to limit the number of professionals involved in a conference to ensure that the family felt that the conference was their own.

## Developing policy and practice in family group conferences

As we have seen, there is a research and evaluation basis for developing FGCs. There is an issue, however, around whether the original FGC model is applied and what the impact of changes to the model may be. For example, the 'grass-roots' approach to the mainstreaming of FGCs in the United States has arguably led to a wide variety of models and the potential dilution of the New Zealand model. For example in Oregon, the FGDM process is not grounded in the New Zealand FGC model as so is not required to include family private time. Vesneski (2009) argues that private time is essential for promoting family decision making but is also one of the only occasions in child welfare when families' decision making is supported by the state and free of its surveillance. With professionals present during the deliberation phase, family members may not feel able to speak freely because it might be used as evidence against them later on. Adams and Chandler (2004) share this concern. They believe variations can be seen as creative adaptations to local conditions but may also compromise the core values of the FGC model. As discussed earlier, this also causes a problem in research; for instance, in one study, two different forms of FGCs are used and, in others, the researcher does not specify what elements of the FGC they used, making it difficult for the reader to analyse the findings (Adams and Chandler 2004).

Another challenge concerns the criteria for referring families to FGC. In most states in America, FGDM rely on referrals by social workers who work on a case-by-case basis. Vesneski (2009) has concerns that this ad hoc way of referring families, coupled with funding variation in supporting families' plans, will affect FGC outcomes. Similarly, one of the reasons that FGCs remain at the margin of family support practice in the United Kingdom is because FGCs there also rely on referrals from social workers. Social workers are only likely to refer if they already believe in the principles of

FGCs: social workers who already strive to work in an empowering way and try to use the philosophy of FGC in their own conferences will now have a better method for putting their principles into practice and families already likely to have a better experience than some will have an even better experience. The social workers who have a more risk-averse, possibly socially controlling approach are unlikely to refer families to an FGC and will use the usual child protection procedures which may be a negative experience for the families (Ghaffar, Manby and Race 2012). Where families are referred to FGC by social workers, only a minority of families will be reached, those fortunate enough to have a social worker who approaches child protection in this way. It will not help those families served by a social worker who does not. In New Zealand, it is a statutory obligation that every family is entitled to an FGC as an alternative to a CPC. Pennell and Burford (2000) argue for a 'trigger' for referrals to an FGC in Canada. Making FGCs part of the law is a big step but Hawaii's approach represents a much smaller step in that direction. For FGCs to become mainstream in the United Kingdom, something like this is required. The Family Rights Group (2011) has similar concerns in the United Kingdom: the provision of FGCs is funded by local authorities and, although the Department for Education supports the use of the model, it is up to individual authorities whether they invest in the service. This leads to what the Family Rights Group calls a 'postcode lottery'. The Family Rights Group has proposed that FGCs should be funded by Legal Aid and should be used in all cases where care proceedings are imminent (Family Rights Group 2011). This would provide the much-needed 'trigger' for FGC referrals and also make them more consistently available throughout the United Kingdom.

The experience of the state of Hawaii in implementing FGC as a model of child welfare reform demonstrates the political support that is required. In reforming child welfare, the Department of Human Services (DHS) faced resistance from child protection workers reluctant to change their practice. To gain the support of these workers, they made FGC training competitive rather than compulsory. Adams and Chandler (2004) report that this had the effect of making it appear a 'scarce commodity' and this attracted people to the training. They then found that the use of FGCs varied geographically, depending on the area management's approach to it. To help combat this, the DHS established goals as to the amount of conferences in an area and published this data, thus encouraging areas to meet the goals. They then followed this up with incentives for social workers, including flexitime and overtime for those attending evening and weekend conferences. Furthermore, a policy was introduced that meant plans agreed in the conference could not be overruled by a supervisor who did not attend the conference. This type of policy is likely to make workers feel more valued and supported and should encourage the use of professional creativity and discretion. Connolly and Smith (2010) suggest that there is reason for social workers to believe that a partnership approach can be of benefit to staff as well as children and families; four years into the child welfare reforms in New Zealand, unallocated reports have decreased by 93 per cent, the number of children in out-of-home care has fallen by 13 per cent since 2006 and frontline staff retention has risen from an average of 5.6 years to 6.7 years since 2005.

Frost (Frost with Elmer 2008) concluded a small local study of FGCs as follows:

1.  The FGCs require expert preparation and facilitation if they are to work well, a process which the coordinator has carried out to an excellent standard.
2.  The system seems to be operating effectively overall in encouraging family participation.
3.  Most conferences were able to draw up an action plan with clear, achievable and agreed aims. After three months, 61 out of 84 agreed action points were actually delivered.
4.  Participation levels at the FGCs have been high. Usually all parties have been able to make active contributions during the meeting.
5.  Older children have been able to contribute, including one instance where a 10-year-old led the feedback following private time.
6.  It is noteworthy that, in almost all cases, very articulate and helpful aunts and uncles (siblings of parents) have emerged as key carers, able to provide concrete assistance to struggling parents. Grandparents have also played a key role.
7.  Review meetings have been held to review the plans and check implementation and progress.
8.  The social workers are pivotal to the FGCs in sharing their assessments with the families. Most social workers have presented these to a high standard, giving a balanced view of the strengths and challenges facing the family. Guidance and training is required for social workers and related professionals as FGCs are developed and become more extensive.
9.  It is important to note that FGCs exist at an interface with other processes – most notably care proceedings, child protection processes and private law processes. This issue is worthy of further research.

---

**Point for reflection:** In what ways can family group conferences be seen as a model for family support practice?

---

## Case Study: Family Group Conferences

*Exercise*
The following scenario can be undertaken as role play or read as a case study.

*Members of the household*
> David – father
> Janine – 10
> Roy – 7

*Significant family members*
David and the children live together in a two-bedroomed house. Charlene, the mother, left two years ago and is suspected to be homeless.
The extended family consists of:

Mary – paternal grandmother
George – paternal grandfather
Kevin – uncle, Dad's brother
Damian – uncle, Dad's brother
Kelly – aunt, Damien's wife
Jane – aunt, Kevin's wife

They have a close friend, Daley, who lives next door.

In attendance at the Conference:

The Chair, the coordinator
Children's social care social worker
Family support worker
Head teacher

*Background*
Charlene, the mother, left the family, with depressive symptoms two years ago and there has been only limited contact since. David, the father, has been struggling to cope ever since. He works long hours and is often exhausted. The children run rings around him, both intellectually and in terms of energy. Daley has been very concerned and contacted social care. He is worried that the children are left alone in the house and that they go to school dirty, smelly and hungry. Dad falls asleep on the settee, leaving the children unsupervised – Daley has seen them playing on the road. All the relatives are concerned, but until the FGC they did not realize how serious the situation was.

The head teacher has raised many issues with Dad and is very concerned about the children. The social worker thought this would be a very good case for an FGC and hopes this will satisfy the head teacher.

*The Chair, the coordinator*   Your role is to facilitate the meeting. Start with introductions and the purpose of the FGC – which is to focus on the best interests of the children. Ask the social worker to introduce the situation, then take any contributions. The professionals then leave the room and ask the family to construct a plan to address what is best for the children.

*Children's social care social worker*   The Chair will ask you to introduce the situation – see the description on the summary sheet. You are determined to keep the family together and support Dad.

*Family support worker*   You want to do what you can to help – you can offer a lot of practical assistance to the family, with transport, after-school and holiday schemes and so on. You are close to the children and you have worked with them.

*Head teacher* You are very worried about this family. You feel that the children are really suffering and are disadvantaged by their situation. They come to school dirty, smelly and hungry. You feel they should be in care.

*Mary, paternal grandmother, and George, paternal grandfather* You are both keen to do what you can to help – but neither of you are very well. You are very worried about the children going into care.

*Kevin, uncle, Dad's brother; Jane, aunt, Kevin's wife* You are a bit critical of David; you think he could do more to help himself. However, you are willing to help by washing the children's clothes.

*Damian, uncle, Dad's brother; Kelly, aunt, Damian's wife* You are both keen to do what you can to help – you can collect the children from school and take them on weekend breaks occasionally.

*Daley, neighbour and friend* You are very worried about the children – you once saw them nearly run over in the road, when David was asleep. You have some sympathy with the head teacher who feels the children may be better off in care.

*David, father* You feel you are doing your best for the children – but you seem to get the blame when It was your wife ran off and them. You work hard – and you get very tired. You clash with the head teacher whom you really dislike.

*Janine, child, 10* This is so embarrassing! Everyone talking about you – and someone said you were smelly and dirty. You just don't want to be there.

*Roy, child, 7* You quite like this – all your relatives are there and you really like your aunts and uncles.

*Case analysis*
This FGC is typical of twelve observed by one of the authors of this book as part of an evaluation. The case study draws on one of these observed studies. In this case, the family network was able to offer support to the father by coming up with a plan to help him care for the children effectively. The case study shows how the family can devise a plan that the professionals are unlikely to come up with – most likely due to a lack of knowledge of the extended family network. There is also a danger that the professionals may assume that the family network is as unable to cope as the household that is the subject of the case study.

## Conclusion

As we have seen in this chapter, family group conferences represent a crucially important element of family support practice at Levels Two, Three and Four of the Hardiker Model. They embody all of the key principles of family support practice that we have outlined in the introduction to this book.

There exists a strong research base underpinning FGCs, although findings are sometimes inconsistent and there is a need for longer-term follow-up studies. We have argued here that the FGC is a crucial element of any comprehensive approach to family support.

## Selected further reading

Frost, N., Abram, F. and Burgess, H. (2013) Family Group Conferences: Evidence, Outcomes and Future Research. Child and Family Social Work, available at doi 10.1111/cfs 12049

Frost, N., Abram, F. and Burgess, H. (2013) Family Group Conferences: Context, Process and Way Forward. Child and Family Social Work, available at doi 10.1111/cfs 12047.

A comprehensive survey of the FGC literature is provided in these two articles. A wide-range of relevant research is outlined and analysed. The authors conclude with suggestions as to how FGC practice can be developed in the future.

Marsh, P. and Crow, G. (1998) *Family Group Conferences in Child Welfare*. Oxford: Blackwell. Marsh and Crow provided one of the early formative books that help spread FGC practice from New Zealand to the United Kingdom and elsewhere. Drawing on original research, whilst dated it still speaks to contemporary practice.

**PART III**

OVERARCHING ISSUES IN DEVELOPING
A SUSTAINABLE APPROACH TO FAMILY
SUPPORT

# 10 Multi-Disciplinary Working: Holistic Work with Families and Children

One of the most significant developments in child welfare since the beginning of the twenty-first century has been the growth of multi-disciplinary working: professionals from different backgrounds working together. This has been of importance to family support but also to other aspects of child welfare – such as practice with looked-after children, in safeguarding and in work with children and young people with disabilities. This chapter explores the growth of multi-disciplinary working, explores underpinning theories and how multi-disciplinary ways of working function in the field of child welfare in general and in the field of family support in particular. It has been maintained throughout this book that, at its best, family support is a multi-disciplinary activity.

## Underpinning theory

Traditionally, child welfare has involved a number of professionals – social workers, doctors, psychologists, therapists, health visitors and play workers, for example. In recent years, there has been a shift of paradigm – from each profession working largely in isolation and communicating only as and when necessary towards multi-disciplinary working being seen as essential and even the default position for professionals. This trend is expressed at its most intense in the form of 'co-location' – where professionals work in a shared office base, which in family support, for instance, might be a children's centre.

There are a number of driving forces behind multi-professional work that can be identified:

1. Many high-profile child death inquiries have found that a common feature contributing to child abuse-related deaths has been poor inter-professional communication, often at the stage where some sort of family support or early help was being offered.
2. It has also been recognized that many social problems facing children, young people and their families are interrelated. Educational opportunity, health, child development and safeguarding, for example, are dependent upon each other. It follows that a holistic, multi-disciplinary approach is required for family support.

3. The expansion of welfare states at the end of the Second World War contributed to an increasing emphasis on efficiency, economy and 'outcomes-based' accountability. Effective multi-disciplinary work was perceived as contributing towards more efficient working.
4. Multi-disciplinary working has been underpinned by a growth in the utilization of Information and Communications Technology, which has facilitated networking, shared databases and information sharing (see Castells 1996).

Whilst the move towards multi-disciplinary work is widespread, there is a further reason why multi-disciplinary working is crucial to the family support field: this is connected to family support itself being a contested, complex and multifaceted field. Thus, whilst psychotherapy may be the domain of psychiatrists and allied professions, there is no such clear professional claim for family support practice. As we have seen in this book, family support involves many fields of work and differing levels of intervention. Thus family support can be seen as involving family therapy, play work, community outreach, day care, social work and home visiting, to name but a few. Thus, no single profession can be identified as 'owning' or dominating family support. As the Welsh government states in relation to its early years 'Flying Start' programme: 'The development of a multi-agency approach to Flying Start is key to the effectiveness of the programme and is instrumental in supporting children and families' (Welsh Government 2012: 7).

Whilst we have conceptualized multi-disciplinary work in terms of professionals working together, there is a further complication in terms of family support: to a certain degree, family support has been de-professionalized. Professionals have vacated the field and it has become dominated by a family support workforce without specific professional qualifications. This issue will be explored further in our next chapter which focuses on workforce development.

## Developing 'communities of practice' for family support

It follows from the lack of professional ownership or single profession domination of the family support discourse that many family support projects and teams are multi-disciplinary in nature. It is maintained here that the concept of 'communities of practice' developed by Wenger and Lave is helpful in understanding how multi-disciplinary teams work together (Lave and Wenger 1991; Wenger 1998).

The concept of 'communities of practice' is complex and evolving (see wenger-trayner.com; Wenger 1998). However, in helping to apply this concept to the family support context, there are three key concepts that Wenger utilizes. Wenger (1998) believes that new knowledge and emerging forms of practice are generated by what he conceptualizes as 'communities of practice'. The process of developing a community of practice is underpinned by three key activities:

- mutual engagement;
- a joint enterprise;
- a shared repertoire.

We will attempt to apply these ideas to the context of family support.

Mutual engagement is how teams work together. For example, in family support this may include running groups, drop-ins or case discussions. Mutual engagement is about working together on shared projects. This concept is particularly helpful in family support which is underpinned by practices involving professionals and sometimes volunteers working together.

A joint enterprise requires having a shared idea about why we are working together and what we are working towards. In family support, this joint enterprise may be:

- supporting families and preventing family problems and breakdown in the geographical area that we work in;
- giving a purpose to the team, enabling members to work together towards a shared goal.

This is important as it will help the team evaluate how it should set priorities and can evaluate the work that it is undertaking.

A shared repertoire shows how 'communities of practice' actually work together. A shared repertoire includes the language, the tools and the techniques and style of our work. When one visits a family support project, one can often learn about the repertoire of the setting by observing issues such as the dress code, the posters on the wall, the 'tools of the trade' that may be in the office or centre. These will give clues about the 'shared repertoire' of the setting.

## Family support: a site of multi-disciplinary work

As we have shown earlier in this chapter, family support is essentially a multi-disciplinary activity because families are not in the remit of any single profession. As Graham Allen argues in his report for the British 2010–2015 coalition government: 'Early intervention can be targeted at just about every problem that now requires a response from modern health, policing and children's services agencies: behavioural and emotional problems, failure to perform well in school, poor parenting (including child protection challenges and major dysfunction in relationships) and anti-social behaviour (including crime)' (Allen 2011: 2).

It is important to note that the taken-for-granted worlds of professionals are social constructs – 'health care', 'social care', 'day care' and other fields of practice have been constructed by the social history and ideological battles between the professions: these professional boundaries are contested, fluid and change overtime. For example, children's social care in England only came into existence in its current form in 2004 after the passage of the Children Act of that year. Prior to that, social work with children was a sub-function of social services departments that worked with people of all ages.

In contrast to these socially constructed, professional boundaries, actual people live their family lives holistically: a child going to school to be educated needs to be healthy, well-fed, looked after and psychologically well to gain from the educational process. The fragmentation of well-being into separate areas of professional expertise is artificial in nature. Given that we have managed to fragment professionals into many specialisms – indeed, the existence of many specialist professions works well as a defining feature of 'late modernity' – we need to try to bring these professionals together to work effectively with children and families.

This is why social work is, perhaps, the key family support profession. The strength of social work is simultaneously its weakness. Social work has an ill-defined or eclectic knowledge base, but its strength is that it can relate to, and act as a bridge between, other professions. As social work draws on sociology, psychology, health and educational theory, for example, it can act to 'cement' together the bricks of the family support 'wall'. For this reason, family support projects are often led by a professional from a social work background. In fact, we can argue that family support is in many ways 'social' work, even though it is carried out across many professional boundaries and by a growing 'para-professional' and volunteer workforce.

## Professional roles in family support

All the major social and health professionals have a role to play in family support. In fact, the engagement of the authors in continuing professional development suggests a sort of professional nostalgia for a return to family support. Many professionals were motivated by a desire to 'help people' to prevent the emergence of social and personal problems: but in the complex and demanding modern world, they find themselves at 'the heavy end', dealing with crisis after crisis in the limited time available. They realize that they are often intervening 'too late' and are dealing with some sort of child protection emergency, where earlier intervention might have helped prevent the problem.

## Health workers

Healthcare practice – particularly public and community health – is based on the premise of universal services and primary prevention. Thus all children – regardless of social class – receive the services of midwives and health visitors. These services are not always conceptualized as such but are nonetheless essential family support services. Other healthcare professionals – occupational therapists, phsyiotherapists, speech therapists, for example – can also play a crucial role in family support. Many of the New Labour-sponsored Sure Start services co-located these crucial healthcare professionals with a range of other professionals, and many of the targets set for Sure Start were health related.

## The 'psy' professions

The French social historian Jacques Donzelot (1979) refers to the 'psy' professions as those who work with individuals and families using psychological and psychiatric methods. Such professions are engaged in family support projects, sometimes being co-located, but perhaps more often as professionals that family support workers can refer to. They will often undertake specialist work at 'secondary', or more often 'tertiary', level with a focus on parenting and/or family functioning. Family therapy techniques, for example, form an important part of the family support service continuum. They enable families to reflect upon and rethink the way they function, often using a 'systems' approach which looks at the context of family life, rather than focusing on individuals (often children) who may be seen as the cause of a family problem.

## Social care professionals

A strong case can be made that the family support function, which from the 1960s until the 1990s belonged firmly to social work, has now been displaced and decentred. The British Seebohm Report, published in 1968, called for a family service and many social workers practised family support in the wake of that report. This was reinforced to a degree by Section 17 of the Children Act 1989 and the subsequent 're-focusing debate'. In the aftermath of the child abuse inquiries and the public and political reaction, social workers were forced more and more into reactive and defensive practice – this in turn can be empirically supported utilizing evidence about the increase in care proceedings following the press coverage of the Baby Peter case, for example. Contemporary state social work operates largely as a child protection service and a service for those children and young people in the care system.

Of course, it is an error to distinguish strongly between 'child protection' and 'family support', as each form of practice often includes elements of the other. This being said, there are few professionally qualified social workers practising exclusively as family support workers. This then has left a vacuum in the field of family support.

## Family support workers

If family support has been vacated by social workers, it is hard to define the new and emerging family support workforce. It is a dispersed workforce, operating in schools, health centres and children's centres. This workforce is dispersed and without a defined professional background. For example, in some local authorities that have closed residential programmes for children, this workforce (often unqualified) has been reorganized into family support teams. In schools, where teachers have had to deal with the consequences of social problems, they have generated teams of 'mentors', 'outreach workers', 'parenting workers' and 'support workers' and so on, who work with children and young people in school and at home in order to mitigate the impact of social problems.

Thus we can see that a range of staff are involved in family support – we could go on to outline just about every human profession and its role in family support. It is a 'decentred' activity, not owned or dominated by any single profession.

> **Point for reflection:** Think about your professional role: which of the above do you fit into? Is the outline role accurate? How could the role of your profession be changed to improve the contribution to supporting families?

## Challenges for multi-disciplinary family support teams

Conceptualizing the family support team as a community of practice does not mean we see it as a haven of harmony and cooperation. We know from the expanding research base on multi-disciplinary teams that they face many challenges. These are identified under eight headings and research findings are applied to the family support field (see Frost 2014 for an extended discussion of these issues):

1.  Complexity and ambiguity: Much of the research on multi-disciplinary teams suggests that the establishment and successful maintenance of such teams is a complex and demanding process. Multi-disciplinary working is never straightforward and needs to be well planned and executed.

2.  Professional identity: Once a wide range of professions are working together closely, whether or not they are co-located, issues arise about professional identity. Traditional profession training and senses of identity are linked to what is specific about that profession and how it is different from other professions. Once the professions are working together, it raises questions about what they have in common and how they can work together most effectively. A strong example is provided by the Common Assessment Framework (CAF). The assessment process was once the 'property' of social work but the CAF suggested that it could be undertaken by any suitably trained professional or para-professional. Thus the issue of professional identity is raised on both sides of the equation: social work could feel threatened by the loss of the assessment process, and other professions may feel threatened by having to undertake this process.

3.  Power, status and difference: Once professionals are working together, for example in a co-located setting, whilst they may share an office and a team name, this does not do away with the long legacy of power and status difference in professional work. Law and medicine are high-status professions which often hold power over other lower-status professions. These differences do not disappear simply because a team is co-located. Of course, other forms of difference are also in play – those of gender and ethnicity, for example.

4.  Leadership: The leadership of multi-disciplinary teams shares features of leadership in single-profession organizations, but it also has specific features and challenges. The leader of a multi-professional team, who is inevitably from one of the professional groups, has to manage a range of professions. He or she will have to gain status and credibility across the range of professions represented in the team and demonstrate that they understand the activities of all the relevant professions and that there is no bias towards their profession of origin. Such leaders can be referred to as 'networked' leaders or 'boundaries crossers'. They need to have skills and capabilities specific to leading multi-disciplinary teams.

5.  Information sharing and communication: One of the most complex and often contested issues in multi-disciplinary working concerns information sharing. The issues of confidentiality and the timing of information sharing are often disputed and complex. Clear information-sharing protocols are required – whether or not staff are co-located.

6.  Outcomes and process: As was discussed in chapter 3, the issue of outcomes is a major point of dispute in family support practice and research. Whilst outcomes are clearly important, we have argued throughout this book that process is important too. However, it is inevitable that service commissioners will want to know what the impacts of multi-disciplinary working in family support actually are. As we have discussed, the outcomes of family group conferences and parenting education programmes are often far from clear.

7.  Structural and organizational issues: Multi-disciplinary working in family support is complex and demanding. Where professionals are co-located it is important that issues such as budgets, record keeping and supervision are carefully planned and agreed. Multi-disciplinary working is more complicated than single-agency working and will require planning and agreement if it is to be effective.

8.  The Team Around the Child: The Team Around the Child (TAC) concept is an essential one when working with children and young people. This idea suggests that professionals should plan their work with a child around the needs of the child, rather than around organizational or bureaucratic boundaries.

## Case study: Multi-Disciplinary Working

*Exercise*
Consider the following case study and the implications for effective multi-disciplinary working.

*Members of the household*
   Tilly – 28, single parent
   Ella – 4
   Nora – 2

*Background*

Tilly is a single parent who has overcome a substance abuse problem but is struggling to cope with her two pre-school children. She is referred to a community-based, multi-professional family support team by her health visitor who is worried that her child care is deteriorating, that she is depressed and that she may revert to her previous substance abuse.

Work with Tilly is coordinated by a key worker whose job title is family support worker. The key worker is a social science graduate but has no professional qualification as such. She sees her role as undertaking an assessment of Tilly and coordinating the support that is required.

The key worker asks a home visitor from the team to provide regular home visits to Tilly. This is a befriending and support role. The home visitor attends about twice a week to talk to Tilly, for around an hour each visit. Tilly and the home visitor talk over a cup of tea about the issues and concerns that Tilly has. The home visitor provides Tilly with a non-judgemental sounding board. This process is something that Tilly looks forward to – it makes her feel valued and listened too. Tilly understands that the process is confidential – the home visitor is only obliged to refer her on if she has child protection concerns.

The key worker has also engaged a drug support worker, who knows Tilly. This worker focuses on substance use and abuse and is experienced in recognizing signs of a return to substance abuse and to the dangers of Tilly's previous networks and social contacts linked to drugs.

The key worker also links Tilly with the project daycare provision. Tilly's two children attend for three mornings per week. This provides the children with play, stimulation and social contact with other children. The daycare workers immediately see an improvement in the cognitive and social achievements of the children.

The daycare provision allows Tilly to attend two of the project activities: the adult education class and the outreach service provided by the Citizen's Advice Bureau. In the adult education class, Tilly gets help with basic literacy and numeracy, with which she has always struggled. This boosts her self-confidence and her prospects of employment. In the advice sessions she also gets advice with the welfare benefits and also legal advice about her problematic relationship with the father of her children.

*Case analysis*

In this brief case study, we can see Tilly's and her children's needs have been addressed holistically. The health visitor, home visitor, daycare workers and substance abuse worker are coordinated by the key worker to provide a multi-disciplinary package of care. This overcomes many of the barriers that are often implicit in the traditional 'silo' approach to working with families. Family support is a partnership approach in two senses – there is the partnership with Tilly, asking her how she perceives her needs and working alongside her, as long as there is no threat to the welfare of her children. In addition, the package of support is a partnership in terms of the professionals working with each other.

## Conclusion

Throughout this book, we have argued that family support is essentially a multi-disciplinary enterprise. Because children and families live interconnected lives, it follows that services should respond in a connected and coordinated manner. Family support includes a wide range of activities, including, for example, community-based activities, play work, therapeutic work, health interventions and counselling. It follows, then, that this will bring workers together from a wide range of different backgrounds and professional qualifications. As we have seen in this chapter, such work is complex and demanding, and it needs to be well organized if we are to deliver responsive and effective services for children, young people and their families.

### Selected further reading

Anning, A., Cottrell, D., Frost, N., Green, J. and Robinson, M. (2010) *Developing Multi-Professional Teamwork for Integrated Children's Services*, 2nd edn. Maidenhead: Open University Press. A book which explores how multi-disciplinary work operates in practice and how this can be understood and theorized.

Lloyd, N. and Harrington, L. (2012) The Challenges to Effective Outcome Evaluation of a National, Multi-Agency Initiative: The Experience of Sure Start. *Evaluation* 18(1): 93–109. An article linking the issue of multi-disciplinarity with evaluation challenges, drawing on the Sure Start experience.

# 11 Developing the Family Support Workforce

All child welfare activities require a trained and supported workforce if they are to be carried out in an efficient, effective and ethical manner. Usually, this is supported and developed by a partnership of employers, universities, professional associations and quality assurance agencies. As a result, child health and welfare professionals – for example, social workers and health visitors – have clear and established methods of becoming qualified and registered to practise. As we shall see in this chapter, this is not the case for the family support workforce where there are specific challenges that need to be addressed if we are to define, develop and support it. Such changes are essential if we are to develop a sustainable approach to family support. This element of child welfare is often underplayed by government, although it is clearly recognized by the Scottish government (2012), which requires 'a confident and competent workforce across all services' as part of its 'Getting it Right for Every Child' programme.

## Underpinning challenges

As has been clear throughout this book, whilst in relation to most child welfare activities we can identify a clear workforce with shared characteristics, this is not the case in terms of the family support workforce. There are two aspects which complicate the identification of the family support workforce: first of all, it is difficult to define and delimit what we understand by family support (see chapters 1 and 2 of this book). Second, the workforce itself comprises diverse elements, working in a variety of settings with different levels of qualification. Let us look at each challenge in turn.

First of all, how can we define family support in terms of the skills required by the workforce? It has been argued throughout this book that family support has the eight features identified in our Introduction. As we have seen earlier, thinking about family support has often adopted what is known as the Hardiker Model (1991) which sees family support as existing at three, or sometimes four, distinct but related levels.

Primary prevention refers to universal programmes, often area-based, working on a voluntary basis with a wide range of families. There should be no stigma attached to using such services and the aim should be to prevent the emergence of family problems. Examples of primary prevention projects may include summer play schemes, adventure playgrounds, toy libraries and children's centres.

Secondary prevention is aimed at families with an identified challenge, who usually recognize these issues themselves and who wish to work with agencies towards change through a support and partnership model. Examples of secondary prevention may include volunteer home-visiting programmes, such as Home-Start.

Tertiary prevention is conceptualized as being at the 'heavier', or perhaps more 'targeted', end of a family support spectrum, thus it may focus on issues such as drug and alcohol abuse or domestic violence.

Quaternary prevention may involve working with children on the 'edge of care', or towards children and young people returning home to their birth parents following a period in care.

Thus family support has a range of diverse characteristics and is practised at a number of different levels, each of which, arguably, requires a different skill set. We can thus perceive how complex the task of developing the family support workforce is.

Having considered exactly what we understand by family support, the next challenge in relation to developing the workforce is to understand who undertakes family support work. There are three segments, it is claimed here, that make up the family support workforce.

1.  First, many professionals undertake work which can be understood as family support. For example, midwives, health visitors, social workers, play workers, daycare workers, and advice workers all undertake activities which may have the features of family support. They hold professional qualifications and professional registration.
2.  Second, there is a cohort of family support workers who fall outside the established professional workforce: they may be outreach workers, family support workers or parenting workers, for example. They tend not to have a defined professional qualification but may well be graduates and/or hold certificates in a range of work with families, children and young people.
3.  Third, family support work is also undertaken by volunteers – people who volunteer in their spare time to undertake a role such as home visiting, normally under the supervision of a member of staff from (1) or (2) above.

Thus the family support workforce is diverse and difficult to define – rather like family support itself. This provides us with a profound challenge in terms of developing and supporting the workforce. In this context, we aim to focus on group (2) above – people who work in family support but for whom there is no universally accepted qualification or career progression framework. To be sustainable, and indeed to flourish in a climate which prioritizes safeguarding, family support requires a trained and supported workforce.

**Point for reflection:** Thinking of your training course or professional activity, how could training and workforce development be improved to make a more significant contribution to family support?

## What does the family support workforce think?

This section of the chapter reports on a survey undertaken by the present authors of the views and perspectives of family support workers – those who fall into group (2) above. These workers took part in two conferences about family support and, as part of the conference process, were asked to complete a short questionnaire. Two key questions were asked:

1. What is the most significant barrier to effective 'early help' in your practice at this moment?
2. Please identify the policy/practice change that would most help develop your 'early help' practice.

Each respondent was allowed to give three 'bullet point' responses to each question: 153 returns were analysed, giving a total of 918 different points. In response to the first question, on barriers to effective practice, five key themes emerged as follows:

- communication and information;
- resources/workforce issues/capacity;
- knowledge/skills;
- context/community/organizational;
- assessment/thresholds.

Each theme is examined in turn below.

## Communication/information barriers to family support practice

A number of participants identified a lack of effective inter-professional working in the family support context: for example, one respondent stated that 'people do not genuinely work together'. Barriers included issues of communication and information sharing: one respondent referred to a lack of 'sharing information to inform working together' and another referred to problems with 'effective communication between areas'. In total, six respondents focused on services and the lack of effective coordination between them as follows:

- 'Services are disjointed'
- 'Barriers and protectiveness between services which limits opportunities for effective collaborative working'
- 'Lack of coordination between services'
- 'Services/practitioners working in isolation'
- 'The 'silo' effect of people working in isolation despite overlapping services'
- '[There is a lack of] agency ownership'

Concerns about multi-professional working often related these barriers to the specific issue of information sharing, with three respondents mentioning policy and protocol shortfalls, referring for example to 'Unclear and different policies regarding information sharing'.

There were also eight respondents who expressed concern about the lack of information on service provision to service users, including 'Lack of information about support available for parents of teenagers' and problems for 'Parents knowing who is out there'. Two participants referred to service users' lack of trust in the services provided: there is a 'lack of engagement by families and avoidance' and a 'lack of trust in services, with a fear of engaging'. Three respondents referred to uneven service provision, conceptualizing this as a 'postcode lottery'.

## Resources/workforce issues/capacity as barriers to family support practice

Unsurprisingly in the austerity environment (the survey was undertaken in late 2012/early 2013 in two large cities), there are concerns about resources and capacity. Some respondents referred to specific projects and a failure to respond to social problems such as a 'reduction of Common Assessment Framework capacity' and 'gaps in specific services, i.e. parenting for parents with teenagers, or Eastern European-speaking workers'.

Others feared that organizations have moved away from universal services and 'family support' towards more targeted services, moving up the tiers of the Hardiker Model. They commented that there are 'high levels of need: families not always referred to children's centres until problems identified and crisis point reached'. Seven referred to specific challenges as follows:

- 'balancing preventative work which would facilitate early help increasingly difficult in constrained budgets and reforms which are impacting on children and families';
- 'funding of non-pathologizing services';
- 'limited help for parents with teenagers';
- 'lack of diverse services';
- 'parenting and family support is not universally available especially for age 5 plus';
- 'services not having time to build quality relationships, time limited';
- 'restrictive criteria which limits access to services'.

In more overarching comments, one respondent referred to a need 'to change the stigma of "family support" perceived as "needing help" to a more encouraging/reassuring method of support/help'. Ten respondents identified concerns with their capacity to respond due to lack of resources, for example stating that 'funding does not allow time and provision to work for families and their needs'.

These funding issues led, of course, to increases in pressure on staff, with seven respondents noting this, for example mentioning having 'large numbers to work with' or a 'strain on the workforce'. Other respondents made more elaborate points about a shortage of resources and pressure on the workforce, believing that '[I]dentifying the children we need to provide early help to sufficiently early will always be a major issue. It is not clear how we pick up children in families where the parents avoid services' and also referencing the need to 'ensure a focus on vulnerable families not "quick wins".'

### Lack of knowledge/skills as a barrier to family support practice

Some participants focused on the lack of staff skills and knowledge as a barrier to effective service delivery, with seven respondents raising issues in relation to this as follows:

- 'knowledge of acute staff about community resources/different job titles';
- 'lack of recognition of the early cognitive development in a child's life and the importance of this and early intervention';
- 'staff who lack confidence and competence can fail to signpost or support families into services';
- 'access and lack of cultural competent services';
- 'staff in family support are not given the level of training that social care gets';
- 'shared assessment/training';
- 'big gap in thinking as often early help equates to early years for some agencies – this isn't the case if engagement is with older age range. However this makes family intervention harder if lead agency is unclear of whom to bring in or signpost to'.

### Contextual, community and organizational barriers to family support

Some participants raised 'big' questions about policy, the social environment and organizational issues. A number of these were about the changing nature of families and of childhood challenges: four referred to issues about working with increasingly 'diverse' and 'complex' families. Four linked this issue specifically to ethnic diversity: 'The changing nature of ethnic minority populations is a challenge to all services. How do we help families where we don't speak the language and don't link to that community?'Another referred to the danger of '[j]udging the community without talking to the community'. Other respondents raised a range of complex and demanding issues on this topic around organizational and community problems, including 'different targets set for differing organizations' and 'different areas covered by different organizations'.

## Assessment/thresholds as barriers to family support

Some of our practitioner respondents addressed the challenging issue of thresholds and assessment, referring to problems around there being 'too many hoops to jump through regarding assessment', and another referred to 'lengthy assessment processes'. Three expressed concerns about repeated assessments, mentioning for example '[h]olistic family plans that are shared and move through tiers – build on plans – don't start again'; 'Don't get "hung up" on same assessment – work to a consistent family plan – whoever is in the house/significant others'. Another respondent commented that there was 'too much focus on outcomes, not process'.

We can see here a wide range of barriers to developing effective family support practice as identified by the 'grass-roots' family support workforce. Having explored the challenges to developing effective practice, participants were then asked which policy and/or practice change would most help to develop their early help practice. The themes are often the reverse of the barriers identified above and are analysed using the same categories as those in our section on barriers.

## Improving family support practice through effective communication and information

Some participants identified relating to improved information exchange and communication as important in improving their practice: six respondents referred to 'effective information sharing policy and implementation' as an essential support for improved family support practice and the need for 'linking information sharing systems'. This would need to be underpinned by an 'effective, informative and rigorous information-sharing process with agreed protocols with *all* agencies'

The need to improve communication more generally was an issue for six respondents as well, calling, for example, for 'more sharing of information from top down' and 'better information for families and workers'.

Some respondents wanted more effective multi-agency working, including co-location of workers and, in particular, '[b]etter communication on key transition points for children, i.e. 5 years, 11 years, 16 years, 18 years of age'.

## Improving family support through resources, workforce issues and capacity

Many of the respondents, unsurprisingly, identified more resources as needed for an improvement in service delivery, with ten respondents commenting:

- 'more resources at local level';
- 'better resources for early years services, recognition in poverty strategy';
- 'budgets which meet the needs of the most vulnerable'.

There was some emphasis, from four respondents, on the need for more universal, family support services, including arguing that 'parenting and family support should be offered to all new parents as a universal offer'.

## Improving knowledge and skills in family support practice

Staff training and workforce development were seen as important tools in service development by six respondents making the following comments:

- 'Better training is required for staff and volunteers';
- 'Better training [is needed] for family support workers, especially around communication skills and how to engage sensitively with parents'.

Some respondents made points relating to parenting education, including 'making parenting a part of the GCSE syllabus' and working for 'non-violence in parenting'.

## Improving the context, community and organizational environment for family support

Five respondents made points regarding the wider context of their work concerned with improving multi-disciplinary collaboration, calling for 'better integrated systems', 'joint working across key services' and 'synchronized geographical services'. Nine respondents emphasized enhanced partnership working with parents and families, with more 'family involvement in service delivery', mentioning 'using family resources, keeping control within families [and] ownership of plans within families'. Other respondents raised overarching policy issues, including a 'more strategic lead and direction' and the need for 'new regulations and legislation'. Even more widely, one respondent called for a 'cultural shift in social structure'.

## Assessment and thresholds: improving family support practice

Ten respondents suggested methods of improving practice around assessment and the application of thresholds, four suggesting a unification of systems through a 'common shared assessment process' and 'better pathways to referral through a single route'.

## Discussion of issues arising from the survey

We can see that there emerged a wide range of diverse responses to the questions posed by the family support workforce. The task of leadership and workforce development teams is to take these issues forward into actions plan that will enhance 'early help' and 'family support' for children and young people. In summary, the major themes emerging from the collated responses from the family support workforce survey are the need:

- for improved inter-agency working;
- for improved methods of information sharing between agencies;
- for improved information provision for professionals and parents;
- to protect and develop universal forms of family support;
- for additional resources;
- for enhanced staff training;
- to continue to recognize diversity amongst communities; and
- to enhance assessment processes.

The future of a sustainable approach to family support is dependent on addressing these issues and developing policy alongside a coherent workforce development.

## Developing the family support workforce

The shift – both intended and unintended – in recent approaches to family support has left us with a dilemma. We have argued throughout this book that family support has been displaced from established professions, notably social work, to become a dispersed and diverse workforce.

This dilemma requires a strategic approach as taken by the Yorkshire and Humberside Workforce Leads Group (2013) in their policy document, *Professional Capabilities Framework for the Wider Children's Workforce: Early Intervention and Prevention.* This document draws on the Professional Capabilities Framework (PCF) for social workers and adapts it in a sophisticated manner for the family support workforce which it identifies as the 'wider children's workforce'.

The document identifies the skill set required by the workforce as follows:

> To identify early signs of potential unequal outcomes for particular children and young people, and provide the support needed to deliver the best possible outcomes for each child, the practitioners that make up the workforce will need to develop a consistent and professional approach. Effective early intervention means recognising, assessing and working with the spectrum of needs that children and young people present, right through to and including the interface with social care at the point of referral for 'child in need' (Section 17) and 'child in need of protection' (Section 47). (Yorkshire and Humberside Workforce Leads Group 2013)

The document is aimed at all stakeholders in relation to the family support workforce as follows:

- service commissioners to support the articulation of the services and workforce needed to address the needs of local children, young people and their families;
- training and development providers to identify the learning and development needs of the wider children's workforce;
- strategy leads, service managers and team leaders to support a strategic commitment to embed the widening of frontline delivery of prevention and early intervention to all staff, whether they work in the statutory,

health, private or voluntary sectors. Senior managers will be able to use this framework for workforce planning and as the basis of the quality assurance of practice in early intervention and prevention work to improve outcomes for children and young people. It will also help team leaders and service managers to be clear about their expectations for the workforce so they can support and challenge them effectively;

- HEI providers to understand the needs of employers and students in work on early intervention and prevention;
- Individuals to further their personal and professional development. It will help those in both the children's and adult workforce to recognize and improve their skills in promoting the well-being of and safeguarding of children across the spectrum of need. It will also ensure that the workforce are safe to take on their responsibilities to support the children, young people and families that they work with. (Yorkshire and Humberside Workforce Leads Group 2013)

This functional approach is underpinned by a helpful statement of values:

- Children and young people value practitioners who enjoy working with them, who treat them with respect and who are good at communicating with them.
- Children's practitioners place the interests of children at the heart of their work. They share responsibility for a range of outcomes for children. They are committed to ensuring all children have a childhood (including protection from harm), are educated, are healthy, are treated fairly and are heard (including considering children's views). They recognize children's fundamental right to be safe in order to reach other goals.
- Practitioners concern themselves with the whole child, whatever their specialism. Although their own involvement with specific children may be short term, children's practitioners work to develop the potential and capacities of children for the longer term.
- Children's practitioners are committed to equality of opportunity for all children, and actively combat discrimination and its effects through their work. They respond positively and creatively to diversity among children and families, and colleagues.
- Practitioners recognize that respect, patience, honesty, reliability, resilience and integrity are valued by children, families and colleagues. By demonstrating these qualities in their work, they help to nurture them in others. (Yorkshire and Humberside Workforce Leads Group 2013)

It also draws on a number of approaches to professional learning and workforce development as follows:

- the development of practitioners' confidence, underpinned by experience and reflective practice;
- increasing the ability of practitioners to work independently and with initiative;
- ensuring that practitioners maximize the opportunity for coordinated

effort across services and collaborate effectively with other professionals;
- improving the quality of the judgements that professionals make through their ability to effectively identify evidence, analyse it and use the findings to inform their decision making;
- encouraging practitioners to engage effectively with complex situations where there are multiple problems, to recognize the significant risk factors within a particular situation and where necessary realize the potential for multi-agency input;
- understanding the appropriate use of support and challenge;
- the commitment to professional supervision and professional development.

The document then uses this approach to provide a framework for developing family support workers through seven different levels of competences and eight areas of practice. This is precisely the type of approach we need if we are to develop an efficient, effective and sustainable family support workforce.

> **Point for reflection:** What do you think of the plans outlined above to improve the family support workforce? How do you think the family support workforce could be further developed?

## Case Study: Developing the Workforce

*Exercise*
Imagine that you were devising a family support team to work in a deprived inner-city area that is ethnically diverse. There are issues with family breakdown, domestic violence, poverty and substance abuse. You have enough funding to employ eight workers: which professions would you choose? Would you select general family support workers or people from professions (such as social workers, health visitors, family therapists)? Provide a rationale for your choice.

*Case analysis*
We have argued throughout this book that family support is a multidisciplinary practice carried out by a workforce that is supported and developed. It is best undertaken by family support workers who focus on this work in particular, or by a range of different established professions working together. The material in this chapter should help you reflect on this issue.

## Conclusion

We can see that if we are to be serious about working with families to support them we require a detailed and sophisticated approach to workforce development such as that proposed by the Yorkshire and Humberside document. This can be mapped against the policy and practice changes desired by the workforce – as represented in the survey which is presented above. The development of the workforce will clearly be crucial to the future of family support.

### Selected further reading

Frost, N. (2014) Children's Services: The Changing Workplace, in P. Foley and A. Rixon, (eds), *Changing Children's Services*. Bristol: Policy Press. A chapter that explores the changing nature of the children's services workplace, drawing on theory and research findings.

# Conclusion:
# Family Support Past,
# Present and Future

In this book, we have attempted to bring together the many strands of family support: history, theory, complex definitions, research base, workforce issues and the application of these to family support practice. We hope that we have made a case for family support as an important and central child welfare practice.

Based in approaches of empowerment, restorative practice and partnership, we believe that family support plays a crucial social role, particularly in times of rapid social, political and economic change which tend to take a heavy toll of families and their children when they are struggling with low pay, unemployment and social marginalization. Family support can be designed utilizing the Hardiker Model (discussed in chapter 1) to ensure services are set at the appropriate level and represent the minimum of stigma.

Raising children in contemporary society is challenging – even if the parent(s) has access to resources to support them in these challenges. A humane and moral society should strive to support parents not only because this will increase the quality of life for families and households, but also because family support, as we have seen, makes social and economic sense (see Featherstone, White and Morris 2014).

We have seen in this book how Victorian organizations, such as the NSPCC and the Charity Organization Society, were formed in the late nineteenth century to challenge the emergence of social and family problems. Clearly, these family support organizations worked within the values of their age: words such as 'feckless', 'immoral' and 'rescue' were used in ways that we would not today. However, they founded some of the basic tools of modern family support, most notably the home visit. Today, those dominant Victorian concepts have been displaced by others, such as 'empowerment', 'partnership' and 'co-production'. The basic aim of preventing social and family problems from emerging or getting worse remains.

We have demonstrated that, in the second decade of the twenty-first century, there are still issues to be challenged and hopefully resolved. We have also explored in this book the tension between family support, early help and early intervention. This conceptual dispute is still open-ended: we have seen that issues around research and evidence remain to be settled.

In this study, we have made the case for family support as a multifaceted activity containing within it a diversity of levels and activities. We advocate family support at all four levels identified – primary, secondary, tertiary and quaternary – which contain the wide range of activities explored in this book, based on the eight features of family support outlined in our introduction. Precisely because family support is a 'slippery concept' – this is problematic – it may also be advantageous in that it allows the concept to embrace and engage complexity and diversity. Any attempt to reduce family support to 'evidence', 'outcomes' and rigorous RCTs should be resisted in order to enable it to remain fluid, flexible and nimble on its feet. This is essential if it is to address the rapidly changing social context in which modern families have to raise their children. Inevitably, evidence tends to look backwards at a time when we need to look to the future.

We have pointed out that family support has been marginalized as a social practice. All three authors of this book have worked as professionals in family support at some stage in their career: as professionals, we have found this to be rewarding and fulfilling. Such career paths are difficult to find today: jobs are often dependent on short-term project funding, making both projects and careers precarious and risky. It is possible for a family support approach to be central to government approaches – this is largely the case in the Republic of Ireland, for example. The policy statement 'Better Outcomes, Better Futures' (2014) demonstrates the Irish government's commitment to family support: 'Parents will experience improved support in the important task of parenting and feel more confident, informed and able' (Department for Children and Youth Affairs 2014).

The displacement of family support has complex and multiple causes.

1.  Family support has been displaced by a focus on child protection and safeguarding. Because of the high public profile of some child deaths, the focus of professionals and politicians has shifted towards 'heavy end' child protection work. Whilst protecting children at home often includes aspects of family support, these tend to be focused on a relatively small number of children who are subject to child protection plans.
2.  A further displacement has been from a qualified social workforce to a dispersed and varied workforce of family support workers based in schools, health centres and children's centres.
3.  Family support also suffers from a lack of professional and theoretical coherence. For example, there is no definitive theory of family support, only a limited literature and no professional associations that can lobby around it.

As a result of these forces and perhaps others we have not discussed, family support is now a Cinderella service, struggling for recognition and resources. We would argue that this produces a massive deficit in the welfare state, a gap that is leaving parents struggling with child rearing in a complex and changing society without the support they require.

Below are eight features of family support which we have put towards a definition:

1. Family support offers inclusive and engaging practices based on the idea of giving support to families and children who feel they require it. Family support is therefore strongly suggestive of partnership, engagement and consent.
2. Such support can be offered early in the life of the child or early in the emergence of the identified challenge facing the family. It is important that family support services are relevant to all children and young people, and not only to younger children.
3. Family support is a proactive process which engages with the parent(s) and/or young person in the process of change. Implicit in the term 'family support' is the suggestion that change can be made within the family network.
4. Family support attempts to prevent the emergence, or worsening, of family challenges.
5. Family support is necessarily based in a theory of change. Any family support intervention should aim to result in some desirable change and draws on a belief that change is achievable.
6. Family support draws on a diverse 'tool kit' of skills and approaches. It attempts to develop and encourage local, informal support networks.
7. Family support also aims to generate wider social change and benefits. Such results may lead to a saving in public expenditure, a decrease in social problems, an improvement in the quality of family life or a reduction in negative measurable outcomes, such as the number of children coming into care.
8. Family support works with children and young people in partnership and encourages and develops their resilience.

We believe the future of family support, as addressed in this book, has to be underpinned as follows:

1. Family support must be a multi-disciplinary undertaking, involving professionals and volunteers alike in working together across traditional boundaries.
2. It continues to be a multifaceted activity – ranging from political campaigning work to family therapy and all forms of practice in between.
3. Family support needs to build a stronger research base – one which is rigorous but also recognizes process as well as outcomes, and qualitative, quantitative and mixed-methods studies.
4. Family support requires a coherent, trained and supported workforce which undertakes sustainable projects with long-term funding.
5. Family support needs to be based on restorative practices, empowerment, partnership and strong respectful relationships.

We hope this book has made a small contribution towards this important task.

# Resources

Useful websites:

### Family Action

https://www.family-action.org.uk/ A very useful website – outlines the experiences of an organization supporting families since 1869.

### Action for Children

http://www.actionforchildren.org.uk/. Originally National Children's Homes and later NCH, Action for Children, this voluntary organization undertakes a wide range of projects and campaigning activities around family support. Particularly strong on issues around neglect and also on policy questions.

### Home-Start

http://www.home-start.org.uk/. The Home-Start website states that it helps 'families with young children deal with whatever life throws at them. We support parents as they learn to cope, improve their confidence and build better lives for their children. The benefits of our support include improved health and well-being and better family relationships.' Founded in 1973, there are now over 300 Home-Starts in the United Kingdom, Germany and Cyprus.

### Barnardo's

http://www.barnardos.org.uk/whatwedo/. Barnardo's provides support to vulnerable children and their families through a range of activities, including campaigning and service provision. Its services include family centres, community-based parenting programmes and targeted family support projects within the 'Troubled Families' initiative. It also provides specialist support for young carers, children at risk of sexual exploitation and children with disabilities. Its website includes links to its extensive and wide-ranging research reports and publications, many of which are free to access.

## NSPCC

http://www.nspcc.org.uk/Inform/informhub_wda49931.html/. The NSPCC is focused on campaigning activity and service provision to end cruelty to children. 'NSPCC inform' is an online information, advice and support hub that includes access to the organization's library catalogue.

## Community Care

http://www.communitycare.co.uk/. The website provides a broad-ranging resource aimed at discussing contemporary issues and promoting excellence in social care. The 'Children' tab leads to news, practice information and opinion on children and family social work and social care. Searching the website using terms such as 'family support' provides access to a range of recent publications including news reports and research studies.

## The Future of Children

http://futureofchildren.org/publications/journals/. An excellent online fully peer-reviewed journal which provides full access to special issues – for example, on Home Visiting research findings.

## *The Guardian*

http://www.theguardian.com/society/. A useful resource for news, comment and debate around contemporary policy developments and social care issues. The 'Society' tab leads to other relevant links such as 'children' and 'child protection'.

## Family and Childcare Trust

http://www.familyandchildcaretrust.org/about-us/. The Family and Parenting Institute merged with the Day Care Trust in 2013 to form this umbrella organization that works to support families to thrive through research, campaigning and information provision. The website provides information about policy developments and current campaigns, as well as coordinating the Family Information Service for parents about childcare provision and family rights.

## Research in Practice

www.rip.org.uk/. A useful website. In particular, see Commissioning Early Help: Using Evidence-informed Practice to Improve Preventative and Early Help Services by Rebecca Godar. This is a readable text which explores the link between research, evidence and commissioning service provision. Includes a range of practical exercises.

## Government Publications

https://www.gov.uk/. This website provides access to a vast range of government publications, including law, policy, guidance, statistics and consultations. The Department for Education provides a 'children's services' link.

## Social Care Institute for Excellence

http://www.scie.org.uk/about/Index.asp/, and http://www.scie.org.uk/publications/elearning/index.asp/. An independent charity that aims to share knowledge about effective practice across social care and social work services. SCIE provides research briefings, practical guidance and examples of good practice. The online database of information includes access to a wide range of health and social care journals. The online Social Care TV channel includes a range of informative and engaging short videos on topics such as parental mental health and child welfare. SCIE have also developed a range of e-learning resources that enable participants to work through case studies and other interactive modules on a range of subjects including poverty, parenting and social exclusion and using play to communicate with children and young people.

## Different jurisdictions within the United Kingdom

The following websites will help the reader explore the differences within the United Kingdom:

Scotland: http://www.scotland.gov.uk/Topics/People/Young-People/gettingitright/about-named-person
Northern Ireland: http://www.ci-ni.org.uk/
Wales: http://www.childreninwales.org.uk/news/news-archive/launch-child-poverty-animations-wesni/
National Children's Bureau: www.ncb.org.uk

# Bibliography

Action for Children (2009) *Backing the Future: Why Investing in Children Is Good for Us All*. London: New Economics Foundation.

Action for Children (2010) *Deprivation and Risk: The Case for Early Intervention*. London: Action for Children.

Action for Children (2012) Available at http://www.actionforchildren.org.uk/our-services/family-support/childrens-and-family-centres/flying-start-wales/.

Adams, P. and Chandler, S. (2004) Responsive Regulation in Child Welfare: Systemic Challenges to Mainstreaming the Family Group Conference. *Journal of Sociology and Social Welfare* 31: 93–116.

Adams, R. (2012) *Working with Children and Families – Knowledge and Contexts for Practice*. Basingstoke: Palgrave Macmillan.

Ainsworth, M. D. S., Blehar, M., Aters, E. and Wall, S. (1978) *Patterns of Attachment: A Psychological Study of the Strange Situation*. Hillsdale: Lawrence Erlbaum.

Aldgate, J., Tunstill, J. and McBeath, G. (1994) *Implementing Section 17 of the Children Act – The First 18 Months*. London: The Stationery Office.

Allen, G. (2011) *Early Intervention: The Next Steps*. London: The Stationery Office.

Allen, G. and Duncan Smith, I. (2008) *Early Intervention: Good Parents, Great Kids, Better Citizens*. London: Centre for Social Justice and the Smith Institute.

Anning, A., Cottrell, D., Frost, N., Green, J. and Robinson, M. (2010) *Developing Multi-Professional Teamwork for Integrated Children's Services*, 2nd edn. Maidenhead: Open University Press.

Audit Commission (1994) *Seen but Not Heard: Coordinating Community Child Health and Social Services for Children in Need*. London: HMSO.

Bailey, D., Raspa, M. and Fox, L. (2012) What Is the Future of Family Outcomes and Family-Centered Services? *Topics in Early Childhood Special Education* 31(4): 216–23.

Bailey, N. (2012) The Listening to Troubled Families Report is an Ethical Failure. *The Guardian*, 25 October. Available at www.theguardian.com/commentisfree/2012/oct/25/listening-to-troubled-families-report/.

Bailey, R. and Brake, M. (eds.) (1975) *Radical Social Work*. London: Edward Arnold.

Ban, P. and Swain, P. (1994) Family Group Conferences. Australia's First Project Within Child Protection. *Children Australia* 19: 19–21.

Barbour, A. (1991) Family Group Conferences. *Social Work Review* 3(40): 16–21.

Barker, S. and Barker, R. (1995) *A Study of the Experiences and Perceptions of Family and Staff Participants in Family Group Conferences*. Bangor: MEDRA Research Group.

Barlow, J. (1999) *Effectiveness of Parent-Training Programmes in Improving Behaviour Problems in Children Aged 3–10 Years*. Oxford: Health Services Research Unit.

Barrett, H. (2010) *Delivery of Parenting Skills Training Programmes: Meta-Analytic Studies and Systematic Reviews of What Works Best*. London: Family and Parenting Institute.

Baumrind, D. (1967) Child Care Practices Anteceding Three Patterns of Preschool Behaviour. *Genetic Psychology Monographs* 75(1): 43–88.

Baumrind, D. (1989) Rearing Competent Children, in W. Damon (ed.), *Child Development Today and Tomorrow*. San Francisco: Jossey-Bass.

BBC News (2010) Department for Education Returns in Coalition Rebrand. 13 May. Available at http://news.bbc.co.uk/1/hi/uk_politics/8679749.stm.

Behlmer, G. K. (1982) *Child Abuse and Moral Reform in England: 1870–1908*. Stanford: Stanford University Press.

Bellfield, C. R., Noves, M. and Barrett, W. S. (2006) *High/Scope Perry Pre-School Program: Cost Benefit Analysis Using Data from the Age 40 Year Follow Up*. New Brunswick: NIEER.

Beresford, P., Croft, S. and Adshead, L. (2008) 'We Don't See Her as a Social Worker': The Importance of the Social Worker's Relationship and Humanity. *British Journal of Social Work* 38(7): 1388–1407.

Berzin, S. C., Cohen, E., Thomas, K. and Dawson, W. C. (2008) Does Family Group Decision Making Affect Child Welfare Outcomes? Findings from a Randomized Control Study. *Child Welfare* 87(4): 35–54.

Biestek, F. (1961) *The Casework Relationship*. London: Allen and Unwin.

Biss, D. (1995) Weighing Up the Limitations of Partnership Policies in Child Protection: Commentary in Thoburn, Lewis and Shemmings. *Child Abuse Review* 4: 172–5.

Blyth, M. (ed.) (2014) *Moving on from Munro: Improving Children's Services*. Bristol: Policy Press.

Bowlby, J. (1979) *The Making and Breaking of Affectional Bonds*. London: Tavistock.

Brandon, M. et al. (2008) The Preoccupation with Thresholds in Cases of Child Death or Serious Injury through Abuse and Neglect. *Child Abuse Review* 17(5): 313–30.

Broadhead, P., Meleady, C. and Delgado, M. (2008) *Children, Families and Communities, Creating and Sustaining Integrated Services*. Maidenhead: Open University Press.

Brown, L. (2003) Mainstream or Margin? The Current Use of Family Group Conferences in Child Welfare Practice in the UK. *Child and Family Social Work* 8(4): 331–40.

Browne, J. (2012) *Families in an Age of Austerity: The Impact of Austerity Measures on Households with Children*. London: Institute for Fiscal Studies.

Butler, P. (2013) Hundreds of Sure Start Centres Have Closed since Election, Says Labour. *The Guardian*. Available at www.theguardian.com/society/2013/jan/28/sure-start-centres-closed-labour/.

Butler-Sloss, Lady Justice (1988) *Report of the Inquiry into Child Abuse in Cleveland*. London: The Stationery Office.

Canavan, J., Dolan, P. and Pinkerton, J. (2000) *Family Support: Direction from Diversity*. London: Jessica Kingsley Press.

Casey, L. (2012) *Listening to Troubled Families*. London: Department for Communities and Local Government.

Castells, M. (1996) *The Network Society*. Oxford: Blackwell.

Center for Social Services Research (2006) The California Title IV-E Child Welfare Waiver Demonstration Study Evaluation: Final Report, in D. Crampton, Research Review: Family Group Decision Making: A Promising Practice in Need of More Programme Theory and Research. *Child and Family Social Work* 12: 202–9.

Centre 4 Excellence and Outcomes (2010a) *Early Intervention: Early Messages from Effective Local Practice 'Call for Evidence'*. London: C4EO.

Centre 4 Excellence and Outcomes (2010b) *Grasping the Nettle: Early Intervention for Children, Families and Communities*. London: C4EO.

Centre for Social Justice (2011) *Making Sense of Early Intervention: A Framework for Professionals*. London: Centre for Social Justice.

Chandler, S. and Giovannucci, M. (2004) Family Group Conferences: Transforming Traditional Child Welfare Policy and Practice. *Family Court Review* 42(2): 216–31.

Charity Organization Society of the City of New York (1883) *Handbook for Friendly Visitors among the Poor*. New York: Putnam.

Child Poverty Alliance (2014) *Beneath the Surface: Child Poverty in Northern Ireland*. Belfast: CPA.

Children's Workforce Development Council (2009a) *Common Assessment Framework for Children and Young People: Practitioners' Guide*. Leeds: CWDC.

Children's Workforce Development Council (2009b) *The Team around the Child and the Lead Professional*. Leeds: CWDC.

Cleaver, H. (1999) *Children's Needs, Parenting Capacity: The Impact of Parental Mental Illness, Problem Alcohol and Drug Use and Domestic Violence on Children's Development*. London: The Stationery Office.

Cleaver, H. (2010) *Children's Needs, Parenting Capacity: Child Abuse, Parental Mental Illness, Learning Disability, Substance Misuse and Domestic Violence*. London: The Stationery Office.

Cohen, S. (2005) *Folk Devils and Moral Panics*, 3rd edn. Oxford: Routledge.

Connolly, M. (2006) Up Front and Personal: Confronting Dynamics in the Family Group Conference. *Family Process* 45(3): 345–57.

Connolly, M. and Smith, R. (2010) Reforming Child Welfare: An Integrated Approach. *Child Welfare* 89(3): 9–31.

Corby, B. (2006) The Role of Child Care Social Work in Supporting Families with Children in Need and Providing Protective Services – Past, Present and Future. *Child Abuse Review* 15(3): 159–77.

Crampton, D. (2006) Research Review: Family Group Decision Making: A Promising Practice in Need of More Programme Theory and Research. *Child and Family Social Work 2007* 12: 202–9.

Crampton, D. and Jackson W. L. (2007) Family Group Decision Making and Disproportionality in Foster Care: A Case Study. *Child Welfare* 86(3): 51–69.

Crittenden, P. M. (2008) *Raising Parents: Attachment, Parenting and Child Safety*. Devon: Willan Publishing.

Crow, G. and Marsh, P. (1997) *Family Group Conferences, Partnership and Child Welfare: A Research Report on Four Pilot Projects in England and Wales*. Sheffield: University of Sheffield Partnership Research Programme.

Cullen, M. A., Strand, S., Cullen, S. and Lindsay G. (2014) *CANparent Trial Evaluation: Second Interim Report*. London: Department for Education.

Cunha, F. and Heckman, J. (2006) *Investing in our Young People*. New York.

Daniel, B. and Wassell, S. (2002) *Assessing and Promoting Resilience in Vulnerable Children*. London: Jessica Kingsley Publishers.

Daniel, B. et al. (2010) *Child Development for Child Care and Protection Workers*. London: Jessica Kingsley Publishers.

Dartington Social Research Unit (2004) *Refocusing Children's Services towards Prevention: Lessons from the Literature*. London: DfES.

Deacon, S. (2011) *Joining the Dots: A Better Start for Scotland's Children*. Edinburgh: The Scottish Government.

Dearden, C. and Becker, S. (2000). *Growing Up Caring: Vulnerability and Transition to Adulthood: Young Carers' Experiences*. London: Youth Work Press.

De Boer, C. and Coady, N. (2007) Good Helping Relationships in Child Welfare: Learning from Stories of Success. *Child and Family Social Work* 12(1): 32–42.

Department for Children, Schools and Families (2010) *Working Together to Safeguard Children*. London: HMSO.

Department for Children and Youth Affairs (2014) Better Outcomes, Better Futures. Available at www.dcya.gov.ie/.

Department for Communities and Local Government (2012) Troubled Families Programme: Progress at December 2012. London: DCLG.

Department for Education (2011) *A Child-Centred System: The Government's Response to The Munro Review of Child Protection*. London: HMSO.

Department for Education (2012) *Characteristics of Children in Need in England: Year Ending March 2012*. London: TSO.

Department for Education and Skills (2003) *Every Child Matters*. London: TSO.

Department for Education and Skills (2004a) *Every Child Matters: Next Steps*. London: TSO.

Department for Education and Skills (2004b) *Every Child Matters: Change for Children*. London: TSO.

Department of Health (1989) *The Care of Children: Principles and Practice in Guidance and Regulations*. London: TSO.

Department of Health (1991) *Children Act 1989: Guidance and Regulations*. London: TSO.

Department of Health (1994) *The Children Act Report 1993*. London: HMSO.

Department of Health (1995) *Child Protection: Messages from Research*. London: TSO.

Department of Health (2000) *Framework for the Assessment of Children in Need and their Families*. London: TSO.

Dillane, J. et al (2001) *Evaluation of the Dundee Families Project*. Scottish Executive. Dundee City Council: NCH Action for Children.

Dolan, P., Canavan, J. and Pinkerton, J. (2000) *Family Support: Direction from Diversity*. London: Jessica Kingsley Press.

Dolan, P., Canavan, J. and Pinkerton, J. (2006) *Family Support and Reflective Practice*. London: Jessica Kingsley Press.

Donzelot, J. (1979) *The Policing of Families*. New York: Pantheon.

Duch, H (2005) Redefining Parent Involvement in Head Start: A Two-Generational Approach. *Early Child Development and Care* 175: 23–35.

Dunst, C. (1985). Rethinking Early Intervention. Analysis and Intervention. *Journal of Developmental Disabilities* 5: 165–201.

Dunst, C. (2000) Revisiting 'Rethinking Early Intervention'. *Topics in Early Childhood Special Education* 20(2): 95–104.

Dynarski, M. and Del Grosso, P. (2008) Random Assignment in Programme Evaluation and Intervention Research: Questions and Answers. *Journal of Children's Services* (September): 9–13.

Easton, C., Featherstone G., Poet, H., Aston, H., Gee, G. and Durbin, B. (2012) *Supporting Families with Complex Needs: Findings from LARC 4*. Slough: NFER.

Easton, C., Gee, G., Durbin, B. and Teeman, D. (2011) *Early Intervention, Using the CAF Process and its Cost Effectiveness: Findings from LARC 3*. Slough: NFER.

Easton, C., Lamont, L., Smith, R. and Aston, H. (2013) *'We Should Have Been Helped from Day One': A Unique Perspective from Children, Families and Practitioners: Findings from LARC 5*. Slough: NFER.

Easton, C., Morris, M. and Gee, G. (2010) *LARC 2: Integrated Children's Services and the CAF Process*. Slough: NFER.

Ermisch, J. and Murphy, M. (2006) Changing Household and Family Structures and Complex Living Arrangements. *Mapping the Public Policy Landscape*. ESRC Seminar Series.

Family Rights Group (1993) *Family Group Conferences*. London: FRG.

Family Rights Group (2011) *Response to Proposals for the Reform of Legal Aid in England and Wales*. London: FRG.

Featherstone, B. (2004) *Family Life and Family Support: A Feminist Analysis*. Basingstoke: Palgrave Macmillan.

Featherstone, B. and Dolan, P. (2010) *Family Support Highlight 225*. London: NCB.

Featherstone, B., Morris, K. and White, S. (2013) A Marriage Made in Hell: Early

Intervention Meets Child Protection. *British Journal of Social Work*, Advance Access, 19 March. Available at http://bjsw.oxfordjournals.org/content/early/2013/03/18/bjsw.bct052/.

Featherstone, B., White, S. and Morris, K. (2014) *Re-inventing Child Protection*. Bristol: Policy Press.

Ferguson, H. (2004) *Protecting Children in Time*. Basingstoke: Palgrave Macmillan.

Ferguson, H. (2011) *Child Protection Practice*. Basingstoke: Palgrave Macmillan.

Field, F. (2010) *The Foundation Years: Preventing Poor Children Becoming Poor Adults*. London: TSO.

Folgheraiter, F. (2003) *Relational Social Work*. London: Jessica Kingsley Press.

Fook, J. (2002) *Social Work: Critical Theory and Practice*. London: Sage.

Fook, J. and Gardiner, F. (2010) *Practising Critical Reflection: A Resource Handbook*. Maidenhead: McGraw Hill/Open University Press.

Forrester, D., Kershaw, S., Moss, H. and Hughes, L. (2008) Communication Skills in Child Protection: How do Social Workers Talk to Parents? *Child & Family Social Work* 13(1): 41–51.

4 Children (2012) *Sure Start Children's Centres Census, Children's Centres over the Last Year and the Implications for the Future*. London: 4 Children.

Freire, P. (1974) *Education: The Practice of Freedom:* London: Writers and Readers Collective.

Frost, N. (1992) Implementing the Children Act in a Hostile Climate, in Carter et al. (eds), *Changing Social Work and Welfare*. Milton Keynes: Open University Press.

Frost, N. (1997) Delivering Family Support: Issues and Themes in Service Development, in N. Parton (ed.), *Child Protection and Family Support: Tensions, Contradictions and Possibilities*. London: Routledge.

Frost, N. (2003) Understanding Family Support: Theories, Concepts and Issues, in N. Frost, A. Lloyd and L. Jeffrey (eds), *The RHP Companion to Family Support*. Dorset: Russell House Publishing.

Frost, N. (2011) *Rethinking Children and Families*. London: Continuum.

Frost, N. (2014) Children's Services: The Changing Workplace, in P. Foley and A. Rixon, (eds), *Changing Children's Services*. Bristol: Policy Press.

Frost, N. and Dolan, P. (2012) The Theoretical Foundations of Family Support, in M. Davies (ed.), *Social Work with Children and Families*. Basingstoke: Palgrave Macmillan.

Frost, N. with Elmer, S. (2008) *An Evaluation of the Family Group Conference Service in South Leeds*. Leeds: Leeds Metropolitan University.

Frost, N. and Parton, N. (2009) *Understanding Children's Social Care*. London: Sage.

Frost, N. and Stein, M. (1989) *The Politics of Child Welfare*. Brighton: Harvester Wheatsheaf.

Frost, N., Abram, F. and Burgess, H. (2013a) Family Group Conferences: Evidence, Outcomes and Future Research. Child and Family Social Work. Available at doi 10.1111/cfs 12049.

Frost, N., Abram, F. and Burgess, H. (2013b) Family Group Conferences: Context, Process and Way Forward. Child and Family Social Work. Available at doi 10.1111/cfs 12047.

Frost, N., Johnson, L., Stein, M. and Wallis, L. (1996) *Negotiated Friendship: Home-Start and the Delivery of Family Support*. Leicester: Home Start UK.

Frost, N., Johnson, L., Stein, M. and Wallis, L. (2000) Home-Start and the Delivery of Family Support. *Children and Society* 14(5): 328–42.

Frost, N., Lloyd, A. and Jeffery, L. (eds) (2003) *The RHP Companion to Family Support*. Lyme Regis: Russell House.

Garrett, P. M. (2009) *Transforming Children's Services: Social Work, Neoliberalism and the 'Modern' World*. London: McGraw-Hill International.

Ghaffar, W., Manby, M. and Race, T. (2012) Exploring the Experiences of Parents and

Carers whose Children Have Been Subject to Child Protection Plans. *British Journal of Social Work* 42(5): 887–905.

Ghate, D., Shaw, C. and Hazel, N. (2000) *How Family Centres Are Working with Fathers.* York: Joseph Rowntree Foundation.

Gibbons, J. (1991) Children in Need and Their Families: Outcomes of Referral to Social Services. *British Journal of Social Work* 21(3): 217–27.

Gibbons, J. (1992) *The Children Act 1989 and Family Support: Principles into Practice.* London: HMSO.

Gilligan, P. and Manby, M. (2008) The Common Assessment Framework: Does the Reality Match the Rhetoric? *Child and Family Social Work* 13(2): 177–87.

Glass, N. (1999) Sure Start: The Development of an Early Intervention Programme for Young Children in the United Kingdom. *Children and Society* 13(4): 257–64.

Glass, N. (2006) Sure Start: Where Did it Come From: Where Is it Going? *Journal of Children's Services* 1(1): 51–7.

Godar, R. (2013) *Commissioning Early Help.* Dartington: Research in Practice.

Gordon, L. (1988) *Heroes of their Own Lives.* London: Virago.

Gove, M. (2010) 'Munro Review of Child Protection: Better Frontline Services to Protect Children'. Letter to Professor Eileen Munro, 10 June. London: DfE.

Gove, M. (2012) 'The Failure of our Current Child Protection System'. Speech at the Institute of Public Policy Research presented at IPPR, 16 November.

Gregg, D. (2010) *Family Intervention Projects: A Classic Case of Policy-Based Evidence.* London: Centre for Crime and Justice Studies.

Hardiker, P. and Barker, M. (1985) 'Client Careers and the Structure of a Probation and After-Care Agency'. *British Journal of Social Work* 15(6): 599–618.

Hardiker, P. and Barker, M. (1988) 'A Window on Child Care, Poverty and Social Work', in S. Becker and S. Macpherson (eds), *Public Issues, Private Pain: Poverty, Social Work and Social Policy.* London: Insight Books.

Hardiker, P., Exton, K. and Barker, M. (1989) *Literature Reviews: Crime Prevention and Prevention in Health Care.* Leicester: University of Leicester.

Hardiker, P., Exton, K. and Barker, M. (1991a) *Policies and Practices in Preventive Child Care.* Aldershot: Gower.

Hardiker, P., Exton, K. and Barker, M. (1991b) Analysing Policy/Practice Links in Preventive Child Care, in P. Carter, T. Jeffs and M. Smith (eds), *Social Work and Social Welfare.* Milton Keynes: Open University Press.

Hardin, M. (1996) *Family Group Conferences in Child Abuse and Neglect Cases: Learning from the Experience of New Zealand.* ABA Center on Children and the Law.

Haringey Local Safeguarding Children Board (2009) *Serious Case Review: Baby Peter.* London: Haringey LSCB.

Hatherley, G. (2011) *Key Issues for the Fourth Assembly.* Cardiff: Research Service for the National Assembly for Wales.

Hearn, B. (1995) *Child and Family Support and Protection: A Practical Approach.* London: National Children's Bureau.

Heckman, J. (2005) The Scientific Model of Causality. *Sociological Methodology* 35(1): 1–9.

Heckman, J., Moon, S. H., Pinto, R. and Savelyev, P. (2009) The Rate of Return of the High/Scope Perry Pre-School Program. Discussion Paper 4533 Bonn: IZA.

Hellincks, W., Colton, M. and Williams, M. (eds) (1997) *International Perspectives on Family Support.* London: Arena.

Hendrick, H. (2003) *Child Welfare, Historical Dimensions, Contemporary Debate.* Bristol: Policy Press.

HM Government (2010) Available at https://www.gov.uk/.../coalition_programme_for_government.pdf.

HM Government (2013) *Working Together to Safeguard Children: A Guide to Inter-Agency Working to Safeguard and Promote the Welfare of Children.* London: DfE.

HM Treasury (2004) *Choice for Parents, the Best Start for Children: A Ten Year Strategy for Childcare*. London: HMSO.

Hollis, F. (1964) *A Psycho-Social Therapy*. New York: Random House.

Holmes, J. (1997) Attachment, Autonomy, Intimacy: Some Clinical Implications of Attachment Theory. *British Journal of Medical Psychology* 70: 231–48.

Home Office (1998) *Supporting Families*. London: HMSO.

Hoover, T. (2005) *The Critical Role of Leadership in Implementing Family Group Decision Making*. Washington: American Humane Association.

Howard, K. and Brooks-Gunn, J. (2009) The Role of Home-Visiting Programs in Preventing Child Abuse and Neglect. *Future of Children* 19(2) (Fall): 119–46.

Howe, D. (1996) Surface and Depth in Social Work Practice, in N. Parton (ed.), *Social Theory, Social Change and Social Work*. London: Routledge.

Howe, D. (1997) Psychosocial and Relationship-based Theories for Child and Family Social Work: Political Philosophy Psychology and Welfare Practice. *Child and Family Social Work* 2(3): 161–9.

Howe, D. (1998) Relationship-based Thinking and Practice in Social Work. *Journal of Social Work Practice* 12(1): 45–56.

Howe, D. (2010) The Safety of Children and the Parent–Worker Relationship in Cases of Child Abuse and Neglect. *Child Abuse Review* 19(5): 330–41.

Howe, D., Brandon, M., Hinings, D. and Schofield, G. (1999) *Attachment Theory, Child Maltreatment and Family Support*. Basingstoke: Palgrave.

Jack, G. (1997) An Ecological Approach to Social Work with Children and Families. *Child and Family Social Work* 2(2): 109–20.

Jeffrey, E. (2003) Moving on from Child Protection, in N. Frost, E. Jeffrey and A. Lloyd (eds), *The RHP Companion to Family Support*. Lyme Regis: Russell House.

Kane, G. A., Wood, V. A. and Barlow, J. (2007) Parenting Programmes: A Systematic Review and Synthesis of Qualitative Research. *Child Care, Health and Development* 33(6): 784–93.

Katz, I. and Pinkerton, J. (2003) *Evaluating Family Support: Thinking Internationally, Thinking Critically*. Chichester: Wiley.

Laming, H. (2009) *The Protection of Children in England: A Progress Report*. London: The Stationery Office.

Lave, J. and Wenger, E. (1991) *Situated Learning*. Cambridge: Cambridge University Press.

Levine, M. (2000) The Family Group Conference in the New Zealand Children, Young Persons and Their Families Act 1989: Review and Evaluation. *Behavioral Sciences & the Law* 18: 517–56.

Lewis, J., Cuthbert, R. and Sarre, S. (2011) What Are Children's Centres? The Development of Children Centre Services, 2004–2008. *Social Policy and Administration* 45: 35–53.

Lindsay, G., Strand, S. and Davis, H. (2011) A Comparison of the Effectiveness of Three Parenting Programmes in Improving Parenting Skills, Parent Mental Well-being and Children's Behaviour, when Implemented on a Large Scale in Community Settings in 18 English Local Authorities: the Parenting Early Intervention Pathfinder (PEIP). *BMC Public Health* 11: 962.

Little, M. (1999) Prevention and Early Intervention with Children in Need: Definitions, Principles and Examples of Good Practice. *Children and Society* (13): 304–16.

Lloyd, N. and Harrington, L. (2012) The Challenges to Effective Outcome Evaluation of a National, Multi-agency Initiative: The Experience of Sure Start. *Evaluation* 18(1): 93–109.

Lord, P., Kinder, K., Wilkin, A., Atkinson, M. and Harland, J. (2008). *Evaluating the Early Impact of Integrated Children's Services: Round 1 Final Report*, Slough: NFER.

Lubin, J. (2009) Are We Really Looking Out for the Best Interests of the Child? Applying the New Zealand Model of Family Group Conferences to Cases of Child Neglect in the United States. *Family Court Review* 47(1): 129–47.

Lucas, P. J. (2011) Some Reflections on the Rhetoric of Parenting Programmes: Evidence, Theory and Social Policy. *Journal of Family Therapy* 33(2): 181–98.

Lundahl, B. W., Nimer, J. and Parsons, B. (2006) Preventing Child Abuse: A Meta-Analysis of Parent Training Programs. *Research on Social Work Practice* 16(3): 251–62.

Lupton, C. (1998) User Empowerment or Family Self-Reliance? The Family Group Conference Model. *British Journal of Social Work* 28(1): 107–28.

Lupton, C. and Nixon, P. (1999) *Empowering Practice? A Critical Appraisal of the Family Group Conference Approach*. Bristol: Policy Press.

Lupton, C. and Stevens, M. (1997) *Family Outcomes: Following through on Family Group Conferences*. Portsmouth: University of Portsmouth.

Lupton, C., Barnard, S. and Swall-Yarrington, M. (1995) *Family Planning? An Evaluation of the Family Group Conference Model*. Portsmouth: SSRIU, University of Portsmouth.

Maccoby, E. E. and Martin, J. A. (1983) Socialisation in the Context of the Family, in E. M. Hetherington (ed.), *Handbook of Child Psychology 4*. New York: Wiley.

Macdonald, G. (2008) Social Work in the UK: A Testing Ground for Trialists. *Journal of Children's Services* 3(1): 27–39.

Macmillan, H. H., Wathan, N., Barlow, J., Fergusson, D., Leventhal, J. and Taussig, H. (2009) Interventions to Prevent Child Maltreatment and Associated Impairment. *The Lancet* 373(9659): 250–66.

Maiter, S., Palmer, S. and Manji, S. (2006) Strengthening Social Worker–Client Relationships in Child Protection Services: Addressing Power Imbalances and Ruptured Relationships. *Qualitative Social Work* 5(2): 161–86.

Marsh, P. and Crow, G. (1998) *Family Group Conferences in Child Welfare*. Oxford: Blackwell.

Maxwell, G. M. and Morris, A. (1992) The Family Group Conference: A New Paradigm for Making Decisions about Children and Young People. *Children Australia* 17(4): 11–15.

Maxwell, N., Scourfield, J., Featherstone, B., Holland, S. and Tolman, R. (2012) Engaging Fathers in Child Welfare Services: A Narrative Review of Recent Research Evidence. *Child & Family Social Work* 17(2): 160–9.

Mayer, B. (2009) Reflections on the State of Consensus-based Decision-making in Child Welfare. *Family Court Review* 47(1): 10–20.

McGuffin, V. (2002) Family Support: Measuring the Benefits to Families. *Child Care in Practice* 8(4): 251–61.

McKeown, K. (2000) *A Guide to What Works in Family Support Services for Vulnerable Families*. Dublin: Department for Health and Children.

Millar, J. and Ridge, T. (2002) Parents, Children, Families and New Labour, Developing Family Policy, in M. Powell (ed.), *Evaluating New Labour's Welfare Reform*. Bristol: The Policy Press.

Miller, W. and Rollnick, S. (2002) *Motivational Interviewing: Preparing People for Change*. New York: Guilford Press.

Mockford, C. and Barlow, J. (2004) Parenting Programmes: Some Unintended Consequences. *Primary Health Care Research and Development* 5(3): 219–27.

Moran, P., Ghate, D. and Merwe, A. (2004) *What Works in Parenting Support? A Review of the International Evidence*. Policy Research Bureau. London: HMSO.

Morgan, P. (1995) An Endangered Species, in M. David (ed.), *The Fragmenting Family*. London: IEA.

Morris, K. (2013) Troubled Families: Vulnerable Families' Experiences of Multiple Service Use. *Child & Family Social Work* 18(2): 198–206.

Morrison, T. (2007) Emotional Intelligence, Emotion and Social Work. *British Journal of Social Work* 37(2): 245–63.

Munro, E. (2004) The Impact of Child Abuse Enquiries since 1990, in N. Stanley and

J. Manthorpe (eds), *The Age of the Inquiry: Learning and Blaming in Health and Social Care*. London: Routledge.

Munro, E. (2008) *Effective Child Protection*. London: Sage.

Munro, E. (2010) Conflating Risks: Implications for Accurate Risk Prediction in Child Welfare Services. *Health, Risk and Society* 12(2): 119–30.

Munro, E. (2011a) *The Munro Review of Child Protection Interim Report: Department for Education*. London: DfE.

Munro, E. (2011b) *The Munro Review of Child Protection: A Child-Centred System*. London: DfE.

Munro, E. and Calder, M. (2005) Where has Child Protection Gone? *Political Quarterly* 76(3): 439–45.

Munro, E. and Musholt, K. (2013) Neuroscience and the Risks of Maltreatment, Children and Youth Services Review. Available at dx.doi.org/10.1016/j.childyouth.2013.11.002.

National Children's Bureau (2012) *Beyond the Cuts, Children's Charities Adapting to Austerity*. London: National Children's Bureau.

Nixon, P., Burford, G., Quinn, A. and Edelbaum, J. (2005) *A Survey of International Practices, Policy and Research on Family Group Conferencing and Related Practices*. National Center on Family Group Decision Making. Englewood: American Humane Association.

Oakley, A., Rajan, L. and Turner, H. (1998) Evaluating Parent Support Initiatives: Lessons from Two Case Studies. *Health Social Care Community* 6(5): 318–30.

Office of the Children's Commissioner (2011) Don't Make Assumptions – Children and Young People's Views of the Child Protection System and Messages for Change. Available at www.childrenscommissioner.gov.uk/content/publications/content_486/.

O'Leary, P., Tsui, M.-S. and Ruch, G. (2013) The Boundaries of the Social Work Relationship Revisited: Towards a Connected, Inclusive and Dynamic Conceptualisation. *British Journal of Social Work* 43(1): 135–53.

Packman, J. and Jordan, B. (1991) The Children Act: Looking Forward, Looking Back. *British Journal of Social Work* 21(4): 315–27.

Parton, N. (1985) *The Politics of Child Abuse*. London: Macmillan.

Parton, N. (1991) *Governing the Family, Child Care, Child Protection and the State*. London: Macmillan.

Parton, N. (1996) Child Protection, Family Support and Social Work: A Critical Appraisal of the Department of Health Research Studies in Child Protection. *Child and Family Social Work* 1(1): 3–11.

Parton, N. (1997) Current Debates and Future Prospects, in N. Parton (ed.), *Child Protection and Family Support: Tensions, Contradictions and Possibilities*. London: Routledge.

Parton, N. (2006) *Safeguarding Childhood: Early Intervention and Surveillance in a Late Modern Society*. Basingstoke: Palgrave Macmillan.

Parton, N. (2012) The Munro Review of Child Protection: An Appraisal. *Children & Society* 26(2): 150–62.

Parton, N. and O'Byrne, P. (2000) What Do We Mean by Constructive Social Work? *Critical Social Work* 1(2): 1–17.

Patterson, G. R., DeBaryshe, B. D. and Ramsey, E. (1989) A Developmental Perspective on Anti-social Behaviour. *American Psychologist* 44: 329–35.

Payne, M. (2014) *Modern Social Work Theory*, 4th edn. Basingstoke: Palgrave Macmillan.

Penn, H. and Gough, D. (2002) The Price of a Loaf of Bread: Some Conceptions of Family Support. *Children and Society* 16(1): 17–32.

Pennell, J. and Burford, G. (2000) Family Group Decision Making: Protecting Children and Women. *Child Welfare* 79(2): 131–58.

Pinkerton, J. and Katz, I. (2003) Perspective through International Comparison in the

Evaluation of Family Support, in I. Katz and J. Pinkerton (eds), *Evaluating Family Support: Thinking Internationally, Thinking Critically*. Chichester: Wiley.

Pinkerton, J., Dolan, P. and Canavan, J. (2004) *Family Support in Ireland Definition and Strategic Intent*. Northern Ireland: Department of Health and Children.

Pithouse, A. (2006) A Common Assessment for Children in Need? Mixed Messages from a Pilot Study in Wales. *Child Care in Practice* 12(3): 199–217.

Pithouse, A., Lindsell, S. and Cheung, M. (1998) *Family Support and Family Centre Services: Issues, Research and Evaluation in the UK, USA and Hong Kong*. Aldershot: Ashgate.

Plimmer, D. and Van Poortvliet, M. (2012) *Prevention and Early Intervention: Scoping Study for the Big Lottery Fund*. London: New Philanthropy Capital.

Pugh, G., De'Ath, E. and Smith, C. (1994) *Confident Parents, Confident Children*. London: National Children's Bureau.

Putti, M. and Brady, B. (2011) From Tea to Sympathy to Optimal Matching of Need: Developing a Shared Vision for a Community Based Family Support Service. *Child Care in Practice* 17(3): 271–84.

Reed, H. (2012*) In the Eye of the Storm: Britain's Forgotten Children and Families. A Research Report for Action for Children, The Children's Society and NSPCC*. London: Landman Economics.

Rein, M. (1983) *From Policy to Practice*. London: Macmillan.

Richards, M. (1987) Developing the Context of Practice Teaching. *Social Work Education* 6(2): 4–9.

Robb, B. (2013) Social Workers Find Little Has Changed, in Community Care, 20 February. Available at www.communitycare.co.uk/articles/20/02/2013/118933/the-munro-report-two-years-on-social-workers-find-little-has-changed.htm/.

Rose, W. (1992) *The Children Act 1989 and Family Support: Principles into Practice*. London: HMSO.

Rosen, G. (1994) *A Study of Family Views of Wandsworth's Family Group Conferences*. Unpublished Research Report, London: Wandsworth Social Services Department.

Ruch, G. (2005) Relationship-based Practice and Reflective Practice: Holistic Approaches to Contemporary Child Care Social Work. *Child and Family Social Work* 10(2): 111–23.

Ruch, G., Turney, D. and Ward, A. (2010) *Relationship-Based Social Work: Getting to the Heart of Practice*. London: Jessica Kingsley Press.

Rutter, M. (2006) Is Sure Start an Effective Preventive Intervention? *Child and Adolescent Mental Health* 11(3): 135–41.

Ryburn, M. (2004) *Planning for Children Here and in New Zealand*. London: FRG.

Sanders, M. (1999) The Triple P – Positive Parenting Program: Towards an Empirically Validated Multilevel Parenting and Family Support Strategy for the Prevention of Behavior and Emotional Problems in Children. *Clinical Child and Family Psychology Review* 2(2): 71–90.

Sanders, M., Mazzuchelli, T. and Studman, I. (2004) Stepping Stones Triple P: The Theoretical Basis and Development of an Evidence-based Positive Parenting Program for Families Who have a Child with Disabilities. *Journal of Intellectual and Developmental Disability* 29(3): 265–83.

Schneider, M., Avis, M. and Leighton, P. (2007) *Supporting Families and Children: Lessons from Sure Start*. London: Jessica Kingsley Press.

Schweinhart, L., Montie, J., Xiang, Z., Barnett, W., Bellfield, C. and Nores, M. (2005) *Lifetime Effects: The HighScope Perry Preschool Study through Age 40*. Ypsilanti: HighScope Press.

SCIE (2005) *The Health and Well-Being of Young Carers*. London: SCIE.

Scottish Government (2010) *The Financial Impact of Early Years Interventions in Scotland*. Edinburgh: Scottish Government.

Scottish Government (2012) A Guide to 'Getting it Right for Every Child'. Available at www.scotland.gov.uk/gettingitright/.

Scottish Government (2014) *Child Poverty Strategy for Scotland - Our Approach - 2014–2017*. Edinburgh: Scottish Government.

Secretary of State for Social Services (1974) *Report of the Inquiry into the Care and Supervision in Relation to Maria Colwell*. London: HMSO.

Sheppard, M., Macdonald, P. and Welbourne, P. (2007) Service Users as Gatekeepers in Children's Centres. *Child and Family Social Work* 13(1): 61–71.

Sinclair, R. Hearn, B. and Pugh, G. (1997) *Preventive Work with Families: The Role of Mainstream Services*. London: National Children's Bureau.

Smith, G. and Cantley, C. (1999) Pluralistic Evaluation, in C. Lupton and P. Nixon (eds), *Empowering Practice? A Critical Appraisal of the Family Group Conference Approach*. Bristol: Policy Press.

Smith, L. (1998) *Essex Family Group Conference Project, Summary Report*. Essex County Council Social Services.

Smith, M. (2009) *Rethinking Residential Care*. Bristol: Policy Press.

Smith, R. (2008) *Social Work and Power*. Basingstoke: Palgrave Macmillan.

Smith, T. (1999) Neighbourhood and Preventative Strategies with Children and Families: What Works? *Children and Society* 13(4): 265–77.

Statham, J. (2000) *Outcomes and Effectiveness of Family Support Services: A Research Review. Issues in Practice*. Institute of Education, University of London.

Statham, J. (2004) *Effective Services to Support Children in Special Circumstances*. Oxford: Blackwell.

Statham, J. and Haltermann, S. (2004) Families on the Brink: The Effectiveness of Family Support Services. *Child and Family Social Work* 9(2): 153–66.

Statham, J. and Smith, M. (2010) *Issues in Earlier Intervention: Identifying and Supporting Children with Additional Needs*. London: DCSF.

Stedman Jones, G. (1976) *Outcast London*. Harmondsworth: Penguin.

Steele, M., Marigna, M., Tello, J. and Johnston, R. (2000) *Strengthening Families, Strengthening Communities: An Inclusive Programme*. London: Race Equality Unit.

Steib, S. (2004) Engaging Families in Child Welfare Practice. *Children's Voice* 13(5): 14–16.

Sundell, K. and Vinnerljung, B. (2004) Outcomes of Family Group Conferencing in Sweden: A 3-year Follow-Up. *Child Abuse and Neglect* 28(3): 267–87.

Sure Start Children's Centres Census (2012) *Developments, Trends and Analysis of Sure Start*. London: DfE.

Sweet, M. and Appelbaum, M. (2004) Is Home Visiting an Effective Strategy? A Meta-Analytic Review of Home Visiting Programs for Families with Young Children. *Child Development* 75(5): 1435–56.

Thoburn, J., Wilding, J. and Watson, J. (2000) *Family Support in Cases of Emotional Maltreatment and Neglect*. London: The Stationery Office.

Thompson, N. (1998) *Promoting Equality: Challenging Discrimination and Oppression in the Human Services*. London: Macmillan.

Thorn, G., Delahunty, L., Harvey, P. and Ardill, J. (2014) *Evaluation of the Intensive Family Support Service*. Cardiff: GSA.

Tickell, C. (2011) *The Early Years: Foundations for Life, Health and Learning*. London: The Stationery Office.

Torgerson, D. and Torgerson, C. (2008) Invited Editorial: Randomized Controlled Trials in Children's Services. *Journal of Children's Services* 3(1): 2–8.

Trevithick, P. (2003) Effective Relationship-based Practice: A Theoretical Exploration. *Journal of Social Work Practice* 17(2): 163–76.

Trivette, C. and Dunst, C. (2005) Community Based Parent Support Programme, in R. E. Tremblay, R. G. Barr and R. DeV. Peters (eds), *Encyclopaedia on Early Childhood*

*Development,* Montreal, Quebec: Centre of Excellence. Early Childhood Development. Available at http://www.child-encyclopedia.com/documents/Trivette-DunstANGxp. pdf.

Tunstill, J. (1995) The Concept of Children in Need: The Answer or the Problem for Family Support? *Children and Youth Services Review* 17(5/6): 651–64.

UNOCINI (2011) *Thresholds of Need Model: Understanding the Needs of Children in Northern Ireland.* Belfast: DHSSPNI.

Utting, D. (1995*) Family and Parenthood: Supporting Families, Preventing Breakdown: A Guide to the Debate.* York: Joseph Rowntree Foundation.

Vesneski, W. (2009) Street-Level Bureaucracy and Family Group Decision Making in the USA. *Child and Family Social Work* 14(1): 1–5.

Waldegrave, H. (2013) *Centres for Excellence?* London: Policy Exchange.

Wastell, D. and White, S. (2012). Blinded by Neuroscience: Social Policy, the Family and the Infant Brain. *Families, Relationships and Societies* 1(3): 397–414.

Webster-Stratton, C. and Taylor, T. (2001) Nipping Early Risk Factors in the Bud: Preventing Substance Abuse, Delinquency and Violence in Adolescence through Interventions Targeted at Young Children. *Prevention Science* 2(3): 165–92.

Weigensberg, E. C., Barth, R. P. and Guo, S. (2009) Family Group Decision Making: A Propensity Score Analysis to Evaluate Child and Family Services at Baseline and After 36 Months. *Children and Youth Services Review* 31(3): 383–90.

Weiss, H. (2003) Foreword, in I. Katz and J. Pinkerton (eds), *Evaluating Family Support: Thinking Internationally, Thinking Critically.* Chichester: Wiley.

Welsh Government (2012) *Flying Start – Strategic Guidance.* Cardiff: Welsh Government.

Welstead, M. (2011) *Child Protection in England – Early Intervention.* University of Buckingham.

Wenger, E. (1998) *Communities of Practice.* Cambridge: Cambridge University Press.

Wigfall, V. (2006) Bringing Back Community: Family Support from the Bottom Up. *Children and Society* 20(1): 17–29.

Williams, F. (2004*) Rethinking Families.* London: Calouste Gulbenkian Foundation.

Williams, J. (1992). *The Children Act 1989: The Public Law.* London: HMSO.

Williams, Z. (2013) This Early Years Educational Underclass is a Handy Moralisers' Myth. *Guardian,* 5 September.

Williams, Z. (2014) Written on the Brain. *Guardian,* 26 April.

Winnicott, D.W. (1965) *The Maturational Process and the Facilitative Environment.* New York: International Universities Press.

Wolfendale, S. and Einzig, H. (2012) *Parenting Education and Support: New Opportunities.* Oxford: Routledge.

Wolstenholme, D., Boylan, J. and Roberts, D. (2008) *Factors that Assist Early Identification of Children in Need in Integrated or Inter-agency Settings.* Research Briefing 27. London: SCIE.

Yorkshire and Humberside Workforce Leads Group (2013) *Professional Capabilities Framework for the Wider Children's Workforce: Early Intervention and Prevention.* Yorkshire and Humberside Workforce Leads Group.

# Index